THE OFFICIAL
PRICE GUIDE
LINENS, LACE
AND OTHER FABRICS

THE OFFICIAL® PRICE GUIDE

LINENS, LACE

AND OTHER FABRICS

ALDA LEAKE HORNER

FIRST EDITION

HOUSE OF COLLECTIBLES · NEW YORK

Important Notice. All of the information, including valuations, in this book has been compiled from the most reliable sources, and every effort has been made to eliminate errors and questionable data. Nevertheless, the possibility of error, in a work of such immense scope, always exists. The publisher will not be held responsible for losses which may occur in the purchase, sale, or other transaction of items because of information contained herein. Readers who feel they have discovered errors are invited to *write* and inform us, so they may be corrected in subsequent editions. Those seeking further information on the topics covered in this book are advised to refer to the complete line of *Official Price Guides* published by the House of Collectibles.

Published by: House of Collectibles
201 East 50th Street
New York, New York 10022

Distributed by Ballantine Books, a division of Random House, Inc., New York, and simultaneously in Canada by Random House of Canada Limited, Toronto.

Text design by Holly Johnson

Manufactured in the United States of America

ISBN: 0-876-37858-0

First Edition: June 1991

10 9 8 7 6 5 4 3 2 1

TO SCOTT, LEIGH, SUSAN, AND FRANCIS SCOTT
FOR THEIR LOVE AND ENTHUSIASTIC ENCOURAGEMENT.

CONTENTS

ACKNOWLEDGMENTS

Working on this book has been a most pleasant task for me. Not only have I enjoyed the hours of research and visits to estate sales, tag sales, shops, shows, and auctions to gather materials and photographs, but I have also enjoyed meeting with the many friendly people who were willing to give me so much of their valuable time. There were shop owners who allowed me to put up my photographic equipment while their customers squeezed around, and there were friends who called to invite me to dinner, suggesting that I bring a camera because they had just unpacked grandmother's trunk. The list is endless and there are many to whom I owe my heartiest thanks and gratitude.

David Lindquist, with whom I have been associated for a number of years, has always had faith in me; he's given me his fullest support and encouragement in my work on this book and in all my other endeavors. Florence (Flo) Neish (who has the fastest iron and ironing board in the South!) has given hours of her time assisting in research; her help has been invaluable. Carla Butler invited me to photograph, ahead of time, merchandise which she was preparing for estate sales; Laura Benedict allowed me to document her grandmother's lace collection; Dotte Evarts loaned me a ten-year run of a periodical for research; Caroline Powell assisted with research on samplers; Kelly McDowell of Lambertville, New Jersey, another lace enthusiast, helped out in that area; Mario and Joanne LaPoma assisted with quilts; Louise deJarnette Jesse of Lively, Virginia, helped with rugs; and many other shop owners in various states also helped to furnish material for this book. Special thanks goes to Camille Zagaroli, a hooked rug expert, for her assistance, and to Dr. Harriet Whitney for helping to pull all this together.

I am indebted to Colleen Callahan, Curator of Costumes and Textiles, The Valentine Museum, Richmond, Virginia, and her staff for their friendly assistance and interest in this project, and for making available the photographs and material for the color section of this book.

My appreciation and thanks also to Dorothy Harris, Editor-in-Chief of House of Collectibles, whose patience and encouragement has made this effort a pleasure.

INTRODUCTION

When we think about handmade textiles in America, we must reflect on centuries of many cultures. Every country that sent settlers to our shores sent with them their special gifts and talents, which continue to influence our culture today. We have many objects from those early days remaining to enrich our lives and our knowledge of how they lived and the difficulties they surmounted. We have continued to use those special gifts and talents in collecting and reproducing the art and crafts of earlier times. The textiles which we collect today create a nostalgia for the simpler times and the *honesty* woven into the very fiber of these creations. We collect them because they are a document of our heritage.

This book was undertaken to appeal to the average collector—one who is still learning and seeking information and would like to have a convenient gathering of material that covers the most popular types of flat textiles for easy reference. It is not intended in any way to be presented as definitive, but to make available quick and concise information to assist you in making educated decisions about textiles. You will find covered in each category the history of the subject; collecting tips; quality and condition keys to help you recognize the collectibility and visual appeal of the subject in relationship to condition; market trends; care and display of the subject; museums; and a bibliography to assist you in further research. Regarding the latter, I do mean *research* since the three most important words in collecting are research, research, research.

This book is about flat textiles, which include linens, laces, quilts, coverlets, rugs, and samplers. Textiles, as dealt with here, are essentially those things made from fibers: cotton, flax, silk, wool, mineral, hemp, jute, and synthetic. They have been spun and woven, knitted, crocheted, embroidered, hooked, and made into lace. I suggest that you read each chapter to appreciate the history and process which goes into the making of each type of textile, and also read the Fibers entry in the "Glossary." This is important because it gives you an understanding of the basic composition of each fabric and how to recognize and test for it in the textile you are researching.

In entering the items in each category, the sale price for each is the actual price which the article sold for or price tag amount attached to the item for sale.

Each item uses the format shown in the following example:

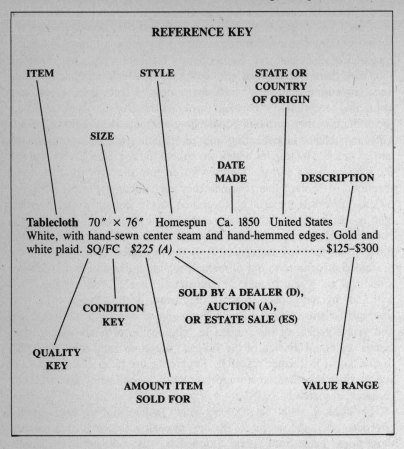

REFERENCE KEY

ITEM   STYLE   STATE OR
                                   COUNTRY
                                   OF ORIGIN

     SIZE

                          DATE
                          MADE   DESCRIPTION

Tablecloth 70″ × 76″ Homespun Ca. 1850 United States
White, with hand-sewn center seam and hand-hemmed edges. Gold and
white plaid. SQ/FC *$225 (A)* .... $125–$300

                          SOLD BY A DEALER (D),
          CONDITION   AUCTION (A),
            KEY   OR ESTATE SALE (ES)

QUALITY
  KEY

        AMOUNT ITEM   VALUE RANGE
        SOLD FOR

The code used for sales source will show A—Auction, D—Dealer, or
ES—Estate Sale (this would include tag sale as same value level).

You will see a price scale as determined by quality and condition. It
is impossible to give any one correct price for any one item, since there
are too many variables which make up the value. Auction prices cannot
be used to determine "fair market" value because, again, too many
variables go into an auction result—weather, proper advertising, timing,
location, lack of interest in the article—and one of the wildest results
may be achieved by having two or more bidders interested in the same
item. I will frequently call an auction house to check on the results of
an item if it is clearly inflated to be sure that it is not a typographical
error, only to find that there were two, and sometimes three, determined
bidding collectors, creating an unrealistic value.

Fair Market Value as defined by the American Society of Appraisers for use in all appraisals as a legal document is: "The price at which the property would change hands between a willing seller and a willing buyer, neither being under any compulsion to buy or sell and both having reasonable knowledge of the relevant facts." To be sure you gain "reasonable knowledge" and understand "relevant facts," therefore, you must research; visit flea markets, auctions, shops, and antiques shows; ask lots of questions; and develop an "eye" for the things you love.

You should also read this book, I might add, and use it on all your shopping sprees. Happy Antiquing!

Linens

HISTORY

This chapter will have both antique and collectible household linens, covering the period from the Victorians up to pre–World War II. Due to the fragile nature of linens and because so many were stored improperly through the years, fewer and fewer of the lovely old pieces are appearing for sale on the market. The finest and earliest will be found in museums and in private collections, and they are not available to the average collector.

However, there is a great interest in linens today, thanks to the many home and decorator magazines and other publications which are showing them being used lavishly in home settings, and the feeling of nostalgia that seems to pervade our culture at this time. There is a tremendous upswing in the manufacture of new linens at present, coming from Europe, China, and also the United States. Some are very well made by hand, although most are machine-made, and they can easily be used with the older pieces.

Most of the newer linens, however, will not show the intricate handwork and the fresh and naive designs that our great-grandmothers and great-aunts lovingly worked into each precious object. Because of this, it is the older linens—those that have, fortunately, survived and have been passed down through the years to us—that we will be discussing here.

We owe much to the banks of the Nile. Not only did the people in that area give us the world's finest long staple cotton, but they also gave us linen from the flax plant. The word "linen" has been borrowed from the Latin *linum* for flax. Linen has been known to exist for many centuries, dating back to wrappings for Egyptian mummies. Linen as a table cover has been mentioned in the Bible and other writings of an early age. We have seen "borde" cloths in early drawings and paintings showing sharply pressed creases in the fold lines. History tells us that tablecloths were in common use among the wealthy in England before the Norman Conquest in 1066. Legend tells us that Huldah the Weaver was an earth goddess in the Tyrolian Alps, and she taught mortals how to grow and weave flax. In summer she would visit the fields and in winter she would check in on the busy housewife, at fireside, to be sure that she was weaving the fruits of the harvest. Every cottage was decorated with dried blue flax flowers at Christmas in her honor.

Today the word "linen" has become a generic designation for our household dressings for the table, bed, kitchen, and bathroom, whether they are made of linen, cotton, lace, silk, or man-made fibers. So, when we refer to "household linens," it can be any of these fibers, and their use will be in the home's adornment and dressing.

During the period in our history before the general use of the fork, when the use of fingers was the accepted means for dining, the napkin was very important. It was very large and usually rectangular. The Romans used them to cover the couch on which they reclined while dining or tied them around their necks. Most guests were expected to bring their own napkin as well as their knife and spoon. The hostess expected the guest to leave his napkin when departing—and he did so if he wished to be invited back! During the period of the elaborate neck ruff, for men as well as women, the large napkin was very necessary for tying around the neck to protect that particular finery. It took some finessing to get the corners of the napkin to reach—hence the expression "making ends meet."

In the early eighteenth century, the napkin went out of vogue for a period of time. The fork had then become the tool of the upper classes who apparently wished to show off their new-found expertise in the use of this new implement. However, after much damage to the edges of tablecloths by sticky fingers, finicky hostesses decided that the napkin was a necessity, to say nothing of a social nicety, and should reappear on the table. There have been recorded some wonderful letters from guests at certain dinners to their families and friends back home who were appalled at the unsightliness of the much used tablecloth edge! Fortunately, the napkin has remained on the table ever since.

Household textiles were a very important part of the furnishings of the home to the early settlers in this country. They were important enough to be mentioned prominently in the inventories of that time, and listings have been made of various cloths, napkins, towels, and other necessities. The family bed, however, was considered the most important single object in the home and, if dressed properly, was certainly the most expensive of the furnishings, worth more than a cow or a horse. The manner in which the bed was dressed reflected the wealth and taste of the owner. When dressed fully, the bed required a tick (mattress), usually of linen or cotton and stuffed with straw, corn husks or leaves; bolsters, pillows, sheets, bedspread or counterpane, blanket, quilt or bed rug; and then all of the necessary hangings if the bed had a tester. All of these things used up many yards of hand-woven linen fabric and required many hours of spinning and weaving to make it possible. Most linen cupboards and chests of that time show locking devices. This was to protect the major investment that their textiles represented.

The Victorians were a leading influence in the development of the great variety of household linens which we see today. They loved finery in all categories and gave us a fancy linen object for every conceivable use. Not only did they love linens, but their love of porcelain is indelibly engraved on our memory with Limoges and other similar porcelain of that period, including those wonderful objects "painted with loving hands on the kitchen table" (also highly collectible today). The lady of the household had time to sit and sew a fine seam—and that she did! She, her daughters, and friends used this as a social activity. Afternoon callers brought their hand-work with them as they came to gossip and take tea. Every young girl was expected to fill her dower chest with exquisitely made linens for her future home and so was taught the art of fine stitchery from an early age. During this period in the nineteenth century, these ladies made some extremely lovely hand-work, which we refer to today as "white work" or "white-on-white," using white embroidery of delicate stitchery, lace insertions, fine tucking, and ruffles on all-white fabric. These are the pieces which are so highly sought after by collectors today. Furthermore, not only did they make these fine household wares, but clothing for women and children as well, and these are very highly collectible today in the vintage clothing market.

My father, a natural storyteller, was the youngest in a family of fourteen and had such wonderful memories of the daily schedule of his mother and older sisters in his family. He told of never seeing his mother or sisters without their work basket beside their favorite chair. The family arrived at the breakfast table at 7:00 A.M. every morning, fully clothed for the day. The morning was filled with correspondence, which was very important in those days before the telephone, menu planning, and piano lessons with their students. Then, after "dinner" at 12:00 noon, they either made ready for callers by 2:00 P.M. or went calling—always having their work basket with them. Never an idle moment!

The early twentieth century saw a decline in that type of fine stitchery. We were entering the period just before World War I and many women were anxious to enter into careers outside the home. They had begun to declare their freedom from home-ties and were fighting for women's suffrage. The social climate was changing rapidly. As the war approached, more were volunteering for the wartime effort. After the war, many women preferred to express their new-found freedom and continued to be interested in careers.

The hand-work done by those ladies who still had time on their hands was beginning to be much more colorful and frivolous, and it did not require long hours of patience to complete. Machine-made lace was now very inexpensive, and pre-stamped embroidery kits using bright silk floss and painted patterns were available as well, as were quilt kits. Some of the popular linens at that time were curtains, bibs, highchair tray covers, tablecloths, vanity sets, and doilies, doilies, doilies. At this time, also, bridge was sweeping the country and hostesses needed cloths and napkins to help entertain in this new vogue. Regarding vanity sets, they, of course, were necessary for that new-style piece of bedroom furniture.

During that dark period of the Great Depression in this country, women had more time at home again. There were very few jobs and the jobs available went to men. Their desire to brighten their homes had them spending more time with handiwork. Among the popular items to come out of the depression era were the crocheted objects, especially bedspreads and tablecloths. Even though crochet had been popular since the late nineteenth century in this country, it really achieved great popularity at this time. Most of the crocheted bedspreads and tablecloths on the market today come from that period, from our mothers' and grandmothers' attics! Most were made with cotton tobacco twine, which was just about as inexpensive as anything they could utilize. Today there are many examples of this craft available and they are highly collectible—they are a real symbol of the age.

With the advent of World War II and the return of women to the job market to replace departing servicemen, the art of stitchery quickly diminished. The new-found technologies and mass production of so many commodities lessened interest in handmade articles.

Fortunately, there is a wave of nostalgia for the old and the beautiful, those things which are not possible with mass production. More and more young people are becoming aware of those linens made during the Victorian era up to about 1940 and are now avid collectors. They, too, are making the rounds of house sales, flea markets, antiques shows, and auctions. Hopefully this book will be helpful!

COLLECTING TIPS

If we are interested in collecting linens, it is important to place these various lovely things in their proper time frame. In that way we can determine, within a period of a few years, if it really is as represented and, considering the three important criteria of quality, condition, and provenance, plus the current market, be able to make an educated decision as to adding it to our collection. What we have to remember is that when given a time period for the introduction of anything—be it textiles, furniture, glass or porcelain—the introduction never started on one given date and then became obsolete on another certain date. That is why we should have some idea of differing time frames for consideration.

We do have documented dates as to when certain machines were invented and registered. However, whatever started in England, France or other European countries usually had a lag time of a few years before reaching our shores. And even in this country, the processes found their way into the hinterlands many years after their introduction into the major cities. It is reasonable to understand that a stylish fad in England certainly did not reach the backwoods of Kentucky or Tennessee until quite a few years later.

So, taking all of these probables into consideration, what do we do when we see a piece which speaks most loudly to us and has no redeeming qualities whatsoever except that we would kill for it? We buy it, take it home, and cherish it no matter what! That one special find is sometimes more exciting than the valuable piece we purchased for investment or to save for our daughter's trousseau some twenty years hence. All of these possibilities make collecting such a joy.

In placing linen collectibles in their proper time frames, the following information should be useful:

• Eighteenth-century homespun is very rare on the market today. Most homespun found at this time is linen and wool in blue checks or plain. Wool was spun and woven in several weights, depending on the intended use. Linen was spun and woven from the fine long fibers of flax for clothing and household linens; tow, the rough end area of the flax plant, was spun and woven into coarse fabric which went into feed sacks and other objects not requiring the finer linen. Most frequently found of the eighteenth-century linens now are bed ticks, bolsters, and pillow cases. Wool hasn't survived as well.

• The spinning jenny was invented by James Hargreaves, an English-

11

man, in 1767, and it could spin sixteen threads at one time. This made weaving of cotton much easier for the housewife. Cotton had not been used to any great extent because of the difficulty in spinning the short fibers, as compared to the longer wool or flax fibers. With the invention of the cotton gin by Eli Whitney in 1793, the weaving of cotton became a reality in this country. However, housewives wove cotton and cotton/linen-blend fabrics using machine-spun threads into the early nineteenth century.

• About 1790, small-print cotton calico was first made in this country. It was usually in two colors and used for clothing and quilts.

• The early nineteenth century saw simple blue or red checks. Brown and color combinations were more rare and are now more valuable.

• Mid-nineteenth century saw the growth of many textile mills and the use of chemical dyes. The latter expanded the production of inexpensive cotton ticking to include stripes of brown, green, and khaki, as well as pinks, raspberry, and a greater selection of reds and blues. Fabrics were being printed with tiny pin dots by 1850.

• Victorian "white work"—all-white cotton or linen with embroidery, tucking, laces, insertions, and ruffles, beautifully worked with minute stitches—was being made by mid-century and was popular into the early twentieth century. This is what we find on the market today in quantities large enough to encourage a collection.

• Late nineteenth century saw the popularity of crochet work and knitting in this country. Victorian white work was now being done with red, as well as brown, embroidery thread. The Japanese influence made its introduction into linen embroidery designs, especially in the screen fan (paddle) motif. Many doilies and cloths show these fans and butterflies in white, as well as in some colors.

• Bright embroidery and appliqués in colors were beginning to become popular in the early twentieth century and continued until the 1930s and 1940s.

• From the period 1910–1920, look for vanity sets and all sorts of lingerie and linen folders, embroidered with such names as "Veils," "Lingerie," "Gloves," "Handkerchiefs," "Napkins," and so on (my favorite has "Corsets"). Dresser sets were very popular at this time also.

• By 1920, bridge was becoming very popular in this country, so look for a great variety of bridge sets. Some will be very lovely and of fine quality, such as Madeira, Appenzell, and Swiss made. However, the market was also flooded with lesser quality sets in kit form, as well as manufactured. Thus, many will be hand-embroidered in bright colors of cotton and silk floss, and many will have machine-made cotton lace edgings. Some made in China and Mexico are very bright and show motifs of their origin. With the advent of bridge sets for one table of four and two tables of eight, we saw the trend away from purchases in quantities of one dozen and one-half dozen napkins, silverware, and table china. Today we rarely see any of these things advertised by the dozen or half-dozen, as was seen early in this century.

• From 1930 on until World War II, you could find all of the items mentioned thus far in cotton and linen, as well as in synthetic mix. Rayon was invented in 1905, but was not named "rayon" until 1927; it soon became available in fabric, laces, and all categories of textiles.

• In the period from 1930–1945, almost every type of household linen came in kit form with a pattern, some complete with pre-stamped fabric and all necessities to complete the project. Almost all were in bright-colored embroidery. From this period, therefore, look for those wonderful tablecloths in bright-printed patterns of fruits, flowers, sail boats, and animals. They come in all qualities, but most often in cotton, synthetic mix, and rayon. They are hot items on the collectible market today and the prices are escalating. This also was the time of brightly printed kitchen towels of the same quality.

When shopping for linens, visit yard sales, flea markets, tag sales, estate sales, and the usual auctions, antiques shops, and shows. There are so many avenues open to collectors that the hunt can be very exciting. Be sure to do your homework first, however, by having some knowledge of what you are most interested in. Museums are a great source of information and most libraries are stocked with all of the necessary references. Owners of legitimate antiques businesses will be most happy to discuss their merchandise and answer your questions. Of course, it helps if you introduce yourself and let the dealer know that you are seriously interested in information. Shopping will be a learning experience for you and hopefully the dealer will be developing a future customer.

At auctions, always look in the box lots. Almost always there will be one or two items which will more than pay for the lot. Last year a major auction house had two box lots of linens with an estimate of $150 each. Apparently there was something very special in each of those boxes, which had escaped the scrutiny of the firm's appraiser, and there were several bidders who were aware of it. The final bid on each was $1,200! If these had been at an estate sale or where each had a set price, someone would have had a banner day. It pays to know what you are shopping for.

If you are collecting for investment, always buy the very finest you can afford and take into consideration *quality*, *condition*, and *prove-*

nance. Be sure to get a written receipt with all of the pertinent information included, and keep accurate and complete files.

The average collector should also consider quality, condition, and provenance, but more latitude is acceptable in selecting things he/she likes but which may need laundering, a simple repair or replacing some of the lace or trim. Such items are meant to be used and enjoyed, and the owner should not be totally desolate if the puppy chews the lace edge off of the pillow cover.

QUALITY AND CONDITION KEYS

CONDITION KEYS

Measures only the physical condition of the article and not the quality of design, material or workmanship.

Fine Condition (FC): Mint, no stains or visible repairs; colors are bright; no thin areas; all lace and trim are intact.

Good Condition (GC): Few repairs which are not obvious; no stains; all seams are strong; colors good.

Average Condition (AC): Some repairs; minor fading; slight thinning; minor spots in fabric; may need new ribbons if applicable; may need laundering.

Poor Condition (PC): Faded; spotting; rips; tears; incomplete. Not collectible, but sections may be used for making doll clothes or other small objects.

QUALITY KEYS

Measures the stylishness and collectibility of the piece within its category.

Good Quality (GQ): Nice piece worthy of collecting, but not for investment.

Very Good Quality (VGQ): Fine fabric and trims, workmanship is excellent; all elements stylistically correct for period.

Superior Quality (SQ): Exquisite fabric and some hand-work; expert workmanship of highest quality; all elements are superb and of the period.

MARKET TRENDS

The trend towards collecting these treasures from the past has escalated in the past several years and seems to be firmly entrenched. There seems to be a plentiful supply of the late nineteenth- and early twentieth-century pieces to keep the market viable for some time to come and to make the search easy as well as fun. Of course, there will always be a market for the museum and top quality linens. This is a good time to shop for top quality pieces because the exquisite trousseaus put together in the early twentieth century, when it was popular for the wealthy to shop in Europe or to commission handmade objects in this country, are now coming into the marketplace through estate sales and from grandmothers' trunks.

There have been a number of publications recently which specialize in all kinds of textiles. Keep a check on the advertisements of firms in major cities and, of course, watch for estate sales, tag sales, small antiques shops, and large antiques shows in your area. There are always bargains to be found if you have done your homework!

CARING FOR
YOUR LINENS

Linens must be laundered and stored with care. The first and most important rule is *never store linens that are not clean and spot free*. The stains or spots may stay there forever. Many antique and collectible linens are fragile and have thinning areas. You may wish to follow some of the suggestions below:

• For fragile or thinning linens, place in tepid water which has mild soap dissolved in it, or use Orvus, a paste cleaning agent (one teaspoon to one gallon of tepid water). Let soak for 30–45 minutes, and then gently remove in a mass, never by an edge, while wet (the weight of the water will cause fraying or tearing). Rinse several times to remove all residue of soap and pat onto a heavy towel to dry flat—never wring or twist.

• Objects which are not too fragile may be laundered in the washing machine on the delicate cycle, using tepid water and the same soap as above. Run through rinse cycle at least twice; the fabric will yellow while ironing if all soap has not been removed. Dry flat in the sun, if possible; otherwise, roll in towels until proper dampness for ironing. I never place any of my linens in the dryer—the heat is deadly!

• Small items should be placed in a mesh bag for protection before being placed in the washer.

• If linens are not fragile, a soaking in mild Clorox II will brighten and refresh tired linens without harm. Be sure to rinse well several times after laundering.

Stain removal is a tricky process requiring patience and care.

• Try sodium perborate, from your druggist, for tough stains and rust. Experiment with proportions according to the severity of the stain. Rinse well and launder as above.

• Era, from the grocery store, works well on blood and other protein stains such as meat juices and gravy. Follow with rinsing and laundering.

• Candlewax must be gently scraped off the surface with the side of a spoon. After removing as much wax as possible, place area on ironing board with a sheet of blotter paper below and one on top. Go over affected area with a warm iron; continue to move area to fresh blotter paper until all residue has been removed. Sometimes a dab of lighter fluid will help with persistent spots. Launder with sodium perborate if the candle has left a colored stain and, as always, rinse well.

When pressing or ironing your linens, best results are obtained if you pad the ironing board well with turkish toweling material and place the top side of the object face down on the board. Any trim or embroidery will stand out in bold relief on the face (if the iron just happens to be too hot, you will also prevent a stain on the face!). When using the iron on trimmed or cutwork pieces, I have found that sliding the iron by its side rather than the point will prevent snagging into the design and causing damage.

Regarding storage of linens, the following hints should prove useful:

• *Never* store linens in plastic bags. They will hold moisture and cause mildew.

• When storing objects which are not used frequently, always put them away unironed and without starch (silverfish just love starch!).

• Storing in a folded position causes the edges not only to become yellow, but will weaken and deteriorate the piece when laundered. Roll in Boy Scout manner and store in a well-laundered pillow case or muslin wrapper (an old sheet works well). Be sure these storage pieces have been rinsed well to remove any trace of soap or detergent.

• Linens which are used often should be wrapped in acid-free tissue and the flat pieces, such as place mats and napkins, may be placed on a shelf which has been padded to cover the wood (wood surfaces have an acid content which will stain textiles).

• For larger pieces, such as tablecloths and runners, use a wooden pole which has been covered with quilted muslin. Roll the cloths on and hold in place with stainless steel quilting pins. Cover with a slip case made from an old sheet and stand the roll in the corner of a closet. There will be no folds to discolor and pressing will be unnecessary when needed for use! Be sure, however, to use stainless steel pins to prevent rusting.

• If a linen cupboard is not available, use acid-free textile storage boxes. The size is convenient to slide under a bed or stack on a closet shelf. Use a plastic envelope attached to the side of the box with an inventory visible for quick retrieval.

LINENS LISTING

Bedspread 94″ × 106″ Candlewick Ca. 1920–1930 United States
Southern. All-white muslin; design of flowers in circles, 3″ fringe on three sides.
Slightly worn. GQ/AC *$35 (ES)*... $25–$75
Bedspread 86″ × 104″ Candlewick Ca. 1930 United States
Southern. Green cotton background; hand-worked candlewick overall in
white polka dots; white fringe on three sides. Faded and worn. GQ/PC *$10
(ES)* .... $10–$50
Bedspread 86″ × 100″ Embroidered Ca. 1930–1935 United States
Unbleached muslin in a single unseamed width; bright colorful pair of peacocks
in cotton floss in center, matching design on bolster area, 4″-wide hem on four
sides. Made from a kit. *(See photo 1)* VGQ/FC *$135 (D)*.............. $50–$150

> This bedspread would make a very striking tablecloth for an informal patio
> meal with small pots of gaily colored flowers around the center motif and
> use of bright pottery dishes.

Bedspread 82″ × 102″ Marseilles Ca. 1890 France
All white; stuffedlike weave in all-over leaf and vine pattern with a center motif
of flowers, ivy, and oak leaves. VGQ/AC *$95 (D)*........................ $50–$195
Bedspread 60″ × 90″ White work Ca. 1880–1890 United States
Victorian, muslin; center decorated with design of fine tucking and insertion of
machine-made embroidered eyelet; edged with ruffle of eyelet trim. VGQ/
FC *$195 (D)* .... $125–$250

PHOTO 1

Bedspread 46" × 62" Appliqué Ca. 1935 United States
Baby bed size; white muslin appliquéd with animals and flowers, touched with embroidery, edged with a band of pale blue fabric. GQ/GC *$65 (D)*. $50–$75

Blanket Double size Beacon Ca. 1930 United States
Cotton flannel; Indian-style design; reds, blues, and grays. North Carolina. Thin and faded. GQ/PC *$10 (ES)*.. $10–$50

Blanket 58" × 60" Pendleton Ca. 1920 United States
All wool; Indian-style design in golds, rusts, and browns. Losses to binding. Thin. GQ/GC *$55 (ES)* .... $25–$75

Blanket 64" × 86" Pendleton Ca. 1930 United States
All-wool blanket or robe; multicolor stripes on a dark red ground. "Beaver State" label. GQ/GC *$95 (A)*... $50–$150

Blanket 62" × 78" Pendleton Ca. 1930 United States
All-wool blanket or robe; special limited edition celebrating the 100th anniversary of Babbit Brothers of Flagstaff, Arizona. Storm pattern in black, red, and white on gray. Original box with labels, etc. VGQ/GC *$165 (A)* ... $100–$250

Blanket 60" × 69" Jacobs Ca. 1930 United States
All-wool blanket or robe; geometric pattern in green, red, white, black, and gold. "Jacob," Oregon City label. VGQ/GC *$192.50 (A)* .... $100–$300

Blanket 68" × 80" Ca. 1850–1860 United States
Early wool blanket; blues, red and white plaid. Two pieces with center seam. Binding is worn, minor wear and moth holes. GQ/PC *$55 (A)*........ $25–$150

Blankets (2) 57" × 72" and 52" × 72" Pendleton Ca. 1930
United States
All-wool blankets or robes; brightly colored designs on turquoise ground; "Beaver State" label. Some wear and fading. One has small hole, and both have moth damage. VGQ/AC *$253 Both (A)*............................ $115–$250 each

> These Indian-style blankets, especially the Pendleton and Jacob, are especially hot on the market at this time in the western part of the United States. One home decorating magazine recently showed these blankets used as drapes, bedspreads, throws, upholstery, and even a sports jacket. Some blankets listed up to $900.

Blanket Cover 76" × 94" Ca. 1935–1940 United States
White rayon crepe, blue satin monogram "bSm" appliquéd in large design in center; blue satin binding, 3" wide, on three sides. GQ/GC *$35 (D)*. $15–$50

Blanket Cover 74" × 90" Ca. 1930 United States
Pale yellow rayon crepe with two rows of 4"-wide ecru lace inserted in side seam lines. GQ/GC *$45 (D)* .... $18–$50

Bolster Case 18" × 60" Ca. 1910–1920 United States
White muslin; open both ends; each end appliquéd with bright blue band and embroidered sprig of flowers. GQ/AC *$15 (ES)*........................... $10–$35

Bolster Case 16" × 58" White work Ca. 1890–1900 United States
Linen, Victorian white work; open both ends, each end scalloped and with heavily padded, embroidered floral design. Minor thin areas. VGQ/AC *$45 (D)*.. $15–$50

Bolster Case 19" × 58½" Ca. 1850–1860 United States
Homespun cover. Navy blue and white plaid with white backing. Hand-sewn. (*See photo 2*) GQ/AC *$170.50 (A)* .... $125–$225

Bridge Set 32" × 32" Ca. 1920–1930 United States
Ivory linen; hand-embroidered with purple grapes and green leaves in shaped

corners, matching center design. Set with four napkins, 12″ × 12″. (*See photo 3*) SQ/FC *$45 Set (D)* .... $25–$50

Bridge Set 33″ × 33″ Appenzell Ca. 1920–1930 Switzerland
White linen, design of narrow drawn work and embroidery in pale blue thread. Set with four napkins, 12″ × 12″. SQ/FC *$50 Set (D)*................. $25–$60

Bridge Set 32″ × 32″ Ca. 1920–1930 United States
White fine linen; embroidered with bright red poppies and green leaves in silk floss. Hemstitched edge. Set with four napkins, 13″ × 13″. Some fading to green floss. (*See photo 4*) GQ/AC *$18.50 (D)*............................. $15–$25

Bridge Set 54″ × 54″ Ca. 1940 United States
Pale pink rayon damask with all-over rose pattern; machine-hemmed. Set with four napkins, 12″ × 12″. GQ/AC *$15 (D)*............................$10–$18.50

Doily 21″ dia. White work Ca. 1890 United States
All-white linen; punch work in spray design with heavy padded, satin stitch embroidered bows. Scalloped edges. (*See photo 5*) VGQ/GC *$40 (D)*...........
.... $20–$65

Doily 24″ dia. Ca. 1920 United States
Ecru linen; floral and leaf design painted on fabric and embroidered around with contrasting colors. Bold work. Edged with heavy machine-made lace. From a kit. Eastern Pennsylvania. (*See photo 6*) GQ/GC *$25 (D)* .... $15–$45

Doily 12″ × 14″ Eyelet Ca. 1940 United States
White cotton; all-over design of machine-made eyelet embroidery. Edged with machine-made eyelet scallops. GQ/AC *$2.50 (ES)* .... $2–$10

Doily 18″ dia. Ca. 1930–1935 United States
White muslin; embroidered roses in bright red silk floss and green leaves. Scalloped edge in green silk floss. Minor fading of green. VGQ/AC *$18.50 (D)*... $15–$35

Doily 12″ × 18″ Cut work Ca. 1900 Italy
Ecru linen; Richilieu (cut work and embroidery) in leaf design. Handmade. SQ/FC *$65 (D)*... $45–$75

THE CONDITION KEY measures only the physical condition of the article and not the quality of design, material or workmanship.

Fine Condition (FC): Mint, no stains or visible repairs; colors are bright; no thin areas; all lace and trim are intact.

Good Condition (GC): Few repairs which are not obvious; no stains; all seams are strong; colors good.

Average Condition (AC): Some repairs; minor fading; slight thinning; minor spots in fabric; may need new ribbons if applicable; may need laundering.

Poor Condition (PC): Faded; spotting; rips; tears; incomplete. Not collectible, but sections may be used for making doll clothes or other small objects.

THE QUALITY KEY measures the stylishness and collectibility of the piece within its category.

Good Quality (GQ): Nice piece worthy of collecting, but not for investment.

Very Good Quality (VGQ): Fine fabric and trims, workmanship is excellent; all elements stylistically correct for period.

Superior Quality (SQ): Exquisite fabric and some hand-work; expert workmanship of highest quality; all elements are superb and of the period.

PHOTO 2

PHOTO 3

PHOTO 4

PHOTO 5

PHOTO 6

PHOTO 7

Fragment 14″ × 88″ Ca. 1860 Russia
Unfinished, fragment of a bedcover, unhemmed edges. Russian Suzini, Usbeck tribe. Hand-woven fabric, natural color background, design is all of needlework in shades of mauve and turquoise. Black and white photograph does not do justice to its beauty. (See photo 7) GQ/AC $325 (D).................. $200–$400

Fragment 30″ × 112″ Homespun Ca. 1850–1860 United States
Piece of homespun linen. Unhemmed. GQ/PC $38.50 (A)............... $25–$65

Fragment 36″ × 42″ Homespun 1836 United States
Piece of homespun linen. Two sides hemmed by hand; one corner embroidered in red "RCB, 1836." Eastern Pennsylvania. GQ/GC $45 (ES) .... $25–$75

Fragments 40″ × 76″ Homespun Ca. 1850–1860 United States
Two pieces, brown and white homespun. Worn, holes, and patched. GQ/PC $93.50 Both (A)................. $50–$125

Handkerchief 11″ × 11″ Appenzell Ca. 1910–1920 Switzerland
Sheer white linen; hemstitched edges; floral design and drawn work in one corner; all done in pale blue thread. VGQ/AC $15 (D)................... $7.50–$25

Handkerchief 12″ × 12″ Ca. 1910–1920 Switzerland
Sheer white linen; hand-embroidered border of small flowers and vines on all four sides, 1″ wide. Edges are scalloped and satin stitched. VGQ/FC $35 (D)................. $25–$50

Handkerchief 12″ × 12″ Ca. 1935–1940 United States
White batiste, overall printed pattern of pink and red roses with green foliage. Machine-hemmed edges. GQ/AC $2.50 (ES)................... $1–$5

Handkerchief 10¾″ × 18″ Ca. 1920 United States
Printed children's handkerchief. Red on white cotton, "Old Mother Hubbard . . . etc." Minor stains, wear, and small holes. Framed. GQ/PC $50 (A)......
.... $10–$65

Handkerchief 11″ × 11″ Ca. 1920 United States
Red and black on cotton with scene of children in goat cart. Stains and hole in one corner. Unframed. GQ/PC $30 (A)................... $5–$35

Handkerchief 17¾″ × 18″ Ca. 1920 United States
Four colorful printed Indian heads and blue border. Not framed. GQ/GC $93.50 (A)................. $35–$125

Handkerchief 14″ × 14¾″ Ca. 1930 United States
Printed. "Boy Scouts of America." Black, gray, and red on white. Minor stains. GQ/AC $33 (A)................... $15–$45

Handkerchief 22″ × 29″ Ca. 1880–1890 United States
Printed, depicting the signing of the Declaration of Independence. Framed. SQ/FC $550 (A)................. $350–$600

Handkerchiefs (2) 14¾″ × 13¾″ Ca. 1920 United States
Two printed handkerchiefs. Red on white cotton. "Birds" and "Wild Beasts." Stains, "Birds" has slight bleeding of color; "Beasts" has repair. In matching frames. GQ/PQ $143 Both (A)................. $30–$65 each

Lingerie Envelope 12″ × 18″ Ca. 1900–1920 United States
White cotton; embroidered with flowers and ribbon bow in heavy-padded satin stitch, tied with pink ribbon (replaced). GQ/AC $35 (D)............... $18–$45

Lingerie Sleeve 9″ × 30″ Ca. 1900–1910 United States
White muslin; embroidered in white and pink flowers and labelled "Corsets" in pink. Drawstring top with pink ribbon (replaced). GQ/AC $27.50 (D).........
.... $15–$45

THE CONDITION KEY measures only the physical condition of the article and not the quality of design, material or workmanship.

Fine Condition (FC): Mint, no stains or visible repairs; colors are bright; no thin areas; all lace and trim are intact.

Good Condition (GC): Few repairs which are not obvious; no stains; all seams are strong; colors good.

Average Condition (AC): Some repairs; minor fading; slight thinning; minor spots in fabric; may need new ribbons if applicable; may need laundering.

Poor Condition (PC): Faded; spotting; rips; tears; incomplete. Not collectible, but sections may be used for making doll clothes or other small objects.

THE QUALITY KEY measures the stylishness and collectibility of the piece within its category.

Good Quality (GQ): Nice piece worthy of collecting, but not for investment.

Very Good Quality (VGQ): Fine fabric and trims, workmanship is excellent; all elements stylistically correct for period.

Superior Quality (SQ): Exquisite fabric and some hand-work; expert workmanship of highest quality; all elements are superb and of the period.

Napkins, Cocktail 5″ × 8″ Ca. 1930 United States
Six, white linen; revelling top-hatted men embroidered on one corner, self-fringed edges. GQ/AC *$12 Set (D)* .... $5–$15

Napkins, Cocktail 8″ × 8″ Ca. 1930–1935 United States
Eight, white linen; small yellow elephants appliquéd in one corner; self-fringed edges. GQ/AC *$15 Set (D)* .... $5–$20

Napkins, Cocktail 5″ × 7″ Ca. 1940 Madeira
Six, lavender linen; bunch of grapes, green linen leaves, cut work, no backing. Handmade. Very unusual. SQ/FC *$45 Set (D)* .... $25–$50

Napkins, Cocktail 9″ × 9″ Ca. 1930 Madeira
Six, white linen; flower basket embroidered in one corner. Scalloped edges. VGQ/GC *$30 Set (D)* .... $25–$45

Napkins, Dinner 22″ × 22″ Ca. 1900 Ireland
Eight, white linen damask; rose pattern, hand-rolled edges. VGQ/GC *$50 Set (D)* .... $35–$65

Napkins, Dinner 28″ × 28″ Ca. 1890 Ireland
Twelve, white linen damask; chrysanthemum pattern, hand-rolled edges; large, padded, satin stitch embroidered monogram ''M'' in one corner. SQ/VGC *$195 Set (D)* .... $150–$250

Napkins, Dinner 24″ × 24″ Ca. 1900 Ireland
Six, white linen damask; center pattern of a wreath, hand-rolled edges. GQ/AC *$65 Set (D)* .... $35–$75

Napkins, Luncheon 14″ × 14″ Ca. 1930 Switzerland
Four, fine white linen; flower basket embroidered in one corner. Scalloped edges. GQ/AC *$15 Set (ES)* .... $10–$25

Napkins, Luncheon 15″ × 15″ Ca. 1935–1940 United States
Four, pale blue rayon damask; floral pattern, machine-hemstitched edges. GQ/AC *$12 Set (D)* .... $9–$15

Napkins, Luncheon 14″ × 14″ Ca. 1940 United States
Four, cream-colored linen; pink cross-stitched rose in one corner, pink embroidered edges. Handmade. GQ/AC *$20 Set (D)* .... $15–$35

PHOTO 8

Piano Throw 90″ × 90″ Ca. 1910–1930 China
White, very fine floral woven silk. Hand-embroidered with white flowers and green leaves in silk floss, 12″ triple-knotted silk fringe on four sides. Minor age stain. (*See photo 8*) SQ/GC *$475 (D)* .... $250–$500

> Quality and workmanship do not affect the condition ranking of an object. The piano throw, for example, is of excellent quality, but unfortunately the value is related to the condition because of minor staining.

Pillow Case 15″ × 17½″ Ca. 1900 United States
Amish, pieced in simple squares and one square of pinwheel pattern in center. Machine-sewn with button back. GQ/AC *$27.50 (A)*...................... $20–$45
Pillow Cases 20″ × 28″ Appenzell Ca. 1900–1910 Switzerland
Pair, fine white cotton, pale blue hemstitching and drawn work with floral designs on each. VGQ/AC *$45 Pair (D)*.. $25–$50
Pillow Cases 22″ × 30″ Ca. 1880–1890 United States
Pair, white linen with heavy-padded satin stitch chrysanthemums and swirls embroidered on each end; ends are scalloped. Minor thinning. (*See photo 9*) VGQ/AC *$35 Pair (ES)*... $25–$45
Pillow Cases 21″ × 29″ Ca. 1930 United States
Pair, white muslin, embroidered with girl in yellow, holding a parasol, surrounded by colorful flowers. Machine-made lace edges. Made from a stamped kit. GQ/AC *$25 Pair (D)*... $18–$35
Pillow Cases 20½″ × 27″ Ca. 1860–1880 United States
Pair, homespun cotton, with pieced and appliquéd quilt square designs in pink and green calico. Designs on both sides, each has a star flower on one side, Carolina lily on other. Minor stains. (*See photo 10*) VGQ/AC *$330 Pair (A)*... $200–$400

PHOTO 9

PHOTO 10

PHOTO 11

PHOTO 12

PHOTO 13A   PHOTO 13B

Pillow Cases 20″ × 28″ Ca. 1890 United States
Pair, fine white linen, hand-sewn and simple hemstitched ends. Inside shows
India ink No. 3. VGQ/AC *$35 Pair (ES)* .... $25–$45
Pillow Cases 22″ × 30″ Ca. 1910–1920 Madeira
Pair, fine white cotton, all-white embroidered flowers, bow ribbons, and swirls.
Machine-made filet lace edging. VGQ/GC *$50 (D)* .... $35–$65
Pillow Sham 28″ × 28″ Ca. 1910–1920 United States
Single, white muslin; embroidered in tan design of leaf and spray; hemstitched
border four sides. Throw type. (*See photo 11*) GQ/GC *$18.50 (D)* .... $15–$35
Pillow Sham 24″ × 36″ Ca. 1885–1900 United States
White muslin with Victorian design in red embroidery of children and dog
in a stream; plants and bird. Throw type, for single bed. This pattern is
shown in several books on Victorian "red work." (*See photo 12*) GQ/AC *$65
(D)* .... $45–$75
Pillow Shams 34″ × 34″ Ca. 1885–1900 United States
White muslin; plain narrow ruffle on four sides. Center design in red embroidery.
One with "Sweet," the other with "Sleep." Throw type. (*See photos 13A and
B*) VGQ/AC *$65 Pair (D)* .... $65–$85
Pillow Shams 25″ × 28″ Ca. 1900 United States
Pair, machine-sewn chain stitch flowers and birds in red and white on white
cotton. Throw type. GQ/GC *$55 (A)* .... $25–$65
Pillow Ticks 23″ × 28″ 1839 United States
Pair, white hand-loomed linen, hand-sewn with minute stitches. "Weltha Wil-
cox, Canaan, Feb. 1839. No. 5" in pale blue minute cross stitch. Narrow hem-
stitched hem, two-pearl button closure at bottom edges. Insect damage on one.
(*See photo 14*) VGQ/AC *$95 (D)* .... $75–$150

PHOTO 14

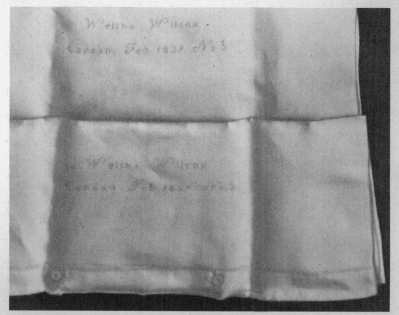

Place Mats 12″ × 18″ Ca. 1940–1945 Portugal
Four; ivory linen of fine quality; left side has appliquéd blue flower with embroidered spray; both ends are scalloped and embroidered in blue; top and bottom edges are hand-rolled. Four napkins in blue, hand-rolled edges 12″ × 12″. Unused, retaining original label of Leacock. SQ/FC *$65 Set (ES)* .... $25–$75
Place Mats 12″ × 18″ Ca. 1935–1940 United States
Four, linen, woven checks of red and tan with self-fringe four sides. Napkins to match, also fringed, 16″ × 15¾″. GQ/AC *$25 Set (D)* .... $15–$35
Place Mats 11″ × 16″ Ca. 1930–1935 Madeira
Four, luncheon size, all-white linen and embroidery of flowers and flower basket. Napkins to match, 12″ × 12″. GQ/GC *$50 Set (D)* .... $35–$65
Place Mats 12½″ × 19″ Ca. 1945–1950 United States
Set, heavy cotton in multicolor stripes, machine-hemmed. Four napkins in red muslin, 18″ × 18″. GQ/AC *$18.50 Set (D)* .... $10–$25
Sheet 84″ × 104″ Bride's Ca. 1920 Madeira
White, fine linen, top end has 18″-deep embroidery in all-white designs of flowers, doves, ribbon bows, and vining. Hand-sewn sides and bottom hem. Beautifully done. SQ/FC *$195 (D)* .... $125–$225
Sheet 84″ × 102″ Ca. 1935–1940 United States
White muslin; heading of sheet has a band of bright embroidery of flowers, leaves, and swirls. Machine-hemmed, possibly from a kit. GQ/AC *$35 (D)* .... $25–$50
Sheet 72″ × 98″ Ca. 1880–1890 Ireland
White linen. Simple design of hand-hemmed 2″ top and narrow-hemmed bottom. Minor thinning. GQ/AC *$25 (ES)* .... $15–$65
Sheet 72″ × 76″ Homespun Ca. 1850–1860 United States
White, homespun. Hand-sewn hems and center seam. Red embroidered initials "M.K." GQ/AC *$44 (A)* .... $15–$65
Sheet 84″ × 102″ Ca. 1945–1950 United States
Set, top sheet, blue percale; top trimmed with 1″-wide rick-rack braid applied with a crochet single stitch. Pair of matching pillow cases with same edge trim and a white, padded satin stitch monogram "S." GQ/AC *$45 (ES)* .. $25–$65
Sheet, Crib 48″ × 54″ Ca. 1930–1940 United States
Top sheet, white muslin. Pale blue band at top and embroidered animals. Matching pillow case, 10″ × 15″. GQ/AC *$45 Set (D)* .... $25–$50
Tablecloth 72″ × 102″ Ca. 1935–1940 Italy
Ecru linen, machine embroidery in brown, and small amount of cut work. Machine-hemstitched edges. With eight matching napkins, 18″ × 18″. (*See photo 15*) GQ/AC *$95 Set (D)* .... $65–$150
Tablecloth 68″ × 98″ Commemorative Ca. 1900 Ireland
Irish linen, double damask. Queen Victoria "Royal Jubilee 1887." Center circular motif showing portrait of the Queen, surrounded by motifs depicting symbols of the countries of the realm interspersed with thistles, elephant, kangaroo, swans, etc. Ribbon motif showing "Royal Jubilee," "1887." Border shows fleur-de-lis, Maltese crosses, background of many small bellflowers. All white. Mint condition. Did not photograph well. SQ/FC *$950 (D)* .... $500–$1,000
Tablecloth 68″ × 116″ Ca. 1920–1940 United States
White cotton damask; "United States Dept. of Navy." Stars, stripes, and rope motif. Institutional quality. GQ/AC *$50 (ES)* .... $35–$95
Tablecloth 92″ × 105″ Ca. 1920 China
White cotton. Center design of drawn work and embroidered floral designs

PHOTO 15

PHOTO 16

with blue threads in the Appenzell manner, but not as fine. Scalloped edges. GQ/AC *$75 (D)* .... $50–$95

Tablecloth 68″ × 104″ Ca. 1940 United States
White muslin. Red cross-stitched design on all four sides, in a floral design. From a kit. GQ/AC *$45 (ES)* .... $25–$65

Tablecloth 54″ × 68″ Ca. 1920 Japan
Pale yellow cotton; bright colored cross-stitch fan and Oriental designs in four corners. Edges done in hand-sewn blanket stitch. Four matching napkins, 14″ × 14″. Not fine. GQ/AC *$45 (D)* .... $25–$50

Tablecloth 70″ × 76″ Homespun Ca. 1850 United States
White, with hand-sewn center seam and hand-hemmed edges. Gold and white plaid. SQ/FC *$225 (A)* .... $125–$300

Tablecloth 72″ × 74″ Homespun Ca. 1880 United States
White homespun cotton with blue and tan plaid borders; hand-sewn edges. (*See photo 16*) GQ/AC *$50 (D)* .... $25–$65

Tablecloth 62″ × 64″ Homespun Ca. 1860 United States
White homespun. Two pieces with decorative stripe design and woven band stitched between halves. Band has traces of red color. Red embroidered initials in corner. Minor stains. GQ/PC *$5.50 (A)* .... $5–$25

Tablecloth 44″ × 62″ Homespun Ca. 1870 United States
Linen, white-on-white woven stripes. Hand-sewn 2″ borders with fringe. GQ/AC *$44 (A)* .... $35–$95

Tablecloth 74″ × 80″ Homespun Ca. 1860 United States
White homespun linen; made in two sections with center seam. A repair. GQ/AC *$27.50 (A)* .... $15–$35

Tablecloth 72″ × 84″ Ca. 1930 Ireland
White linen damask. Rose pattern with oval motif in center. GQ/AC *$18.50 (D)* .... $12–$35

Tablecloth 84″ × 96″ Ca. 1900 Ireland
White linen damask. Floral and ribbon bow pattern. With eight napkins, 22″ × 22″. All pieces machine-hemmed. GQ/AC *$50 Set (D)* .... $25–$75

The CONDITION KEY measures only the physical condition of the article and not the quality of design, material or workmanship.

Fine Condition (FC): Mint, no stains or visible repairs; colors are bright; no thin areas; all lace and trim are intact.

Good Condition (GC): Few repairs which are not obvious; no stains; all seams are strong; colors good.

Average Condition (AC): Some repairs; minor fading; slight thinning; minor spots in fabric; may need new ribbons if applicable; may need laundering.

Poor Condition (PC): Faded; spotting; rips; tears; incomplete. Not collectible, but sections may be used for making doll clothes or other small objects.

The QUALITY KEY measures the stylishness and collectibility of the piece within its category.

Good Quality (GQ): Nice piece worthy of collecting, but not for investment.

Very Good Quality (VGQ): Fine fabric and trims, workmanship is excellent; all elements stylistically correct for period.

Superior Quality (SQ): Exquisite fabric and some hand-work; expert workmanship of highest quality; all elements are superb and of the period.

Tablecloth 64″ × 96″ Ca. 1910–1920 China
White rice cloth. Drawn work and embroidered with roses. Edged in 2″
hemstitched hems. All handmade. Eight matching napkins. GQ/AC *$195*
(D).. $125–$250
Tablecloth 42″ dia. Ca. 1900 United States
White linen. All white work in padded satin stitch, scallop design near center;
border of floral design around outer edge; scalloped border. Minor age discol-
oration. VGQ/AC *$150 (D)* .... $95–$175
Tablecloth 46″ × 46″ Ca. 1930–1940 United States
White coarse cotton; blue check border, blue outlined squares with blue cross-
stitched design in center. Machine-hemmed. GQ/AC *$15 (D)*.......... $10–$25
Tablecloth, Banquet 84″ × 144″ Ca. 1880–1890 Ireland
White, double damask linen. Chrysanthemum pattern, hand-rolled edges,
with twelve matching napkins, 24″ × 24″, hand-rolled edges. SQ/FC *$325*
(D).. $195–$500

In the past few years, the trend has been towards more relaxed and informal
entertaining, so a cloth of this type, which is truly elegant, is finding a smaller
market today. Many can be found on shop shelves and in box lots, however,
and you can find a really great bargain if you scout around. Many, on the
other hand, are being cut into smaller objects, but that really is upsetting and
unacceptable to the serious collector of truly beautiful table linens.

Tablecloth, Kitchen 53″ × 52″ Ca. 1935–1940 United States
All cotton, white background. Blue field with bunches of yellow and pink flowers
with green leaves. Machine-hemmed. GQ/AC *$25 (D)* .... $15–$45
Tablecloth, Luncheon 52″ × 54″ Ca. 1935–1940 United States
White cotton with boldly printed flowers and printed blue border. Machine-
hemmed. GQ/AC *$45 (D)*... $15–$65
Tablecloth, Luncheon 48″ × 48″ Ca. 1930–1940 United States
Printed cotton; boldly colored fruits. Machine-hemmed. GQ/GC *$45 (D)*......
.... $15–$65
Tablecloth, Luncheon 54″ × 53″ Ca. 1935 United States
Printed cotton, gaily colored scenes of black children and adults eating water-
melon. Machine-hemmed. VGQ/GC *$95 (D)*.............................. $25–$95

These gaily printed cloths were very popular in the 1930s and 1940s. Many
were purchased in dime stores, dry goods stores, and department stores.
Made of linen, cotton or cotton and rayon mix, they were modestly priced.
The cloth with the black motif sold for an inflated price because black collectibles are in great demand at present and are not as plentiful as other
textiles. These cloths are now found mostly at flea markets and estate sales.
They are very attractive when used with Depression glassware and Fiesta ware
for patio or other informal entertaining.

Tea Cozy Small size Ca. 1920 England
Insulated flannel-covered liner with two separate white linen covers. Each cover
embroidered with white flowers and having scalloped bottom edge. For two cup-
size pot. Liner has minor interior stains. Covers with label: "Made in England."
VGQ/AC *$35 (ES)* .... $25–$75

PHOTO 17

Towel, Bath 24″ × 40″ Ca. 1980–1990 Ireland
White, double damask linen; gold woven leaf design border; satin stitch monogram "MW" in gold thread, 6″ tied fringe. GQ/AC *$25 (D)* .... $15–$35
Towel, Bath 20″ × 40″ Ca. 1935–1940 Czechoslovakia
White linen damask; 9″ hand-knotted fringe both ends. Unused. VGQ/FC *$35 (ES)* .... $15–$50
Towel, Bath 22″ × 42″ Ca. 1910–1920 United States
White cotton huck; plain woven band each end. GQ/AC *$5 (ES)* .... $5–$15
Towel, Commemorative 19¼″ × 34½″ plus fringe Ca. 1920–1930
United States
Linen, white-on-white woven scene of Washington on horseback. Red border with "Washington." Mint. VGQ/FC *$60.50 (A)* .... $25–$75
Towel, Fingertip 9″ × 13″ Ca. 1940 Mexico
White cotton; bright-colored Mexican designs in cross stitch. Self-fringe both ends. GQ/AC *$5 (D)* .... $3–$10
Towel, Guest 14″ × 24″ Ca. 1935–1949 United States
White linen. One end with band woven in royal blue showing "Our Guest" in white and a daisy on each side. Other end machine-hemmed. *(See photo 17)*
GQ/AC *$15 (D)* .... $2–$20
Towel, Hand 15″ × 23″ Ca. 1890 United States
White linen huck, woven pattern on each end. GQ/AC *$7.50 (ES)* ...... $3–$15
Towel, Hand 17½″ × 25″ Homespun Ca. 1950–1960 United States
Homespun linen, blue and white, hand-hemmed. Wear and small holes.
GQ/PC *$60.50 (A)* .... $25–$75
Towel, Hand 18″ × 24″ Ca. 1920–1930 United States
White linen; embroidered both ends in Oriental designs of orange and blue, 3″ hand-tied fringe both ends. GQ/AC *$12 (ES)* .... $5–$18
Towel, Hand 18″ × 24″ Ca. 1930–1940 United States
White linen huck; plain woven band each end, both ends with monogram "L" in red. Minor stains. GQ/AC *$3.50 (ES)* .... $1–$10
Towel, Hand 18″ × 22″ Ca. 1910–1920 United States
White linen; embroidered in white with Oriental fan and flowers on one end. Self-fringe both ends. GQ/GC *$25 (D)* .... $10–$35

PHOTO 18

Towel, Show 18″ × 60″ Homespun 1838 United States
White homespun linen; drawn work and embroidery in red; "KLD," "1838,"
and "ALD"; self-fringe both ends. (*See photo 18*) SQ/FC *$195 (D)* ....
.... $125–$225
Towel, Show 12″ × 64″ Homespun Ca. 1850–1860 United States
Overshot white-on-white stripes; red embroidered initials "O.W.G." GQ/
PC *$22 (A)* .... $10–$35
Towel, Show 19″ × 47″ Homespun 1856 United States
White homespun; stylized floral embroidery with birds and "Frances Mast 1856."
Red, dark brown, and two shades of gold. Trimmed in machine-made lace and
tied fringe. GQ/GC *$130 (A)* .... $95–$150
Towels, Fingertip 9″ × 14″ Ca. 1935–1940 United States
Pair, linen, one blue, one pink. Self-fringed ends, embroidery of yellow roses
and green leaves on each. GQ/AC *$15 Pair (D)* .... $10–$25
Towels, Fingertip 8″ × 14″ Ca. 1940 Madeira
Pair, fine white linen; floral designs embroidered in pale gray thread. Both ends
are scalloped. SQ/FC *$30 Pair (D)* .... $15–$35
Towels, Kitchen Ca. 1920–1940 Assorted United States
Box lot, white cotton; bright prints of fruits, boats, animals, etc. G–PQ/
G–PC *$5 for 10 (ES)* .... $1–$15
Tray Cover 16″ × 20″ Ca. 1940 United States
Set, light blue linen; embroidered with pale pink roses in left corner. With two
napkins, 14″ × 14″. VGQ/VGC *$35 Set (D)* .... $25–$45
Vanity Set Centerpiece, 15″ × 16″ Ca. 1920–1930 United States
Four pieces; embroidered with black trellis design and flowers in bright colors,
machine-made lace edging. From a kit. (*See photo 19*) GQ/AC *$45 Set (D)* ...
.... $25–$65

Vanity Set Centerpiece, 15″ × 16″ Ca. 1920–1930 United States
White heavy linen; embroidered in bright colors; edged with narrow crochet.
Five pieces. From a kit. (*See photo 20*) GQ/AC *$50 (D)*................ $35–$65
Vanity Set Centerpiece, 10″ × 20″ Ca. 1935–1940 United States
White linen with all royal blue embroidery with bonnet girls. Four pieces. From
a kit. (*See photo 21*) GQ/AC *$35 (D)* .... $25–$50

PHOTO 19

PHOTO 20

PHOTO 21

MUSEUMS

When planning to visit a museum, be sure to call ahead and check the days and hours when they are open to the public to view your special interest. Some show only by appointment for individual, as well as guided, tours. It would be very disappointing to travel several hundred miles and arrive, only to find the museum closed on that particular day.

Many museums offer an indentification clinic at given times during the year. Watch for their announcements if you have an item which you wish to document. The fees are usually nominal.

There are many fine museums around the country—too many to list here. Those listed below are just a sampling and a suggestion for your further research.

Daughters of the American Revolution (DAR) Museum
1776 D Street, N.W.
Washington, DC 20006

Museum of Early Southern Decorative Arts (MESDA)
Winston-Salem, NC 27108

National Museum of History and Technology
Smithsonian Institution
Washington, DC 20006

Rockwood Museum
610 Shipley Road
Wilmington, DE 19809
(Open by appointment only)

The Valentine Museum
1015 East Clay Street
Richmond, VA 23219

BIBLIOGRAPHY

Bath, Virginia Churchill. *Needlework in America, History, Designs and Techniques*. New York: The Viking Press, 1974. Covers just about all facets. Well illustrated and has many fine color plates.

Belden, Louise Conway. *The Festive Tradition, Table Decoration and Desserts in America, 1650–1900*. New York: W.W. Norton, A Winterthur Book, 1983. Besides having a wonderful collection of early recipes and a history of table appointments, it also includes a history of table linens.

Buchanan, Rita. *A Weaver's Garden*. Colorado: Interweave Press, 1987. How to raise fiber plants, dye, spin, and weave. Notes square footage of space required to plant for several projects.

Caulfeild, S.F.A. and Blanche C. Saward. *Encyclopedia of Victorian Needlework*. 2 vols. New York: Dover Publications, Inc., reprint 1972 (originally published by A.W. Cowan, London, 1882). Wonderfully illustrated in the Victorian manner and contains just about everything you would ever want to know about Victorian needlework!

Dolan, Maryanne. *Old Lace & Linens, Including Crochet, An Identification and Value Guide*. Florence, AL: Books Americana, Inc., 1989. Paperback, 156 pages. This has quite a few illustrations and values of early twentieth-century linens and laces, but has little text or specific identification.

Finch, Karen, O.B.E. and Greta Putnam. *The Care and Preservation of Textiles*. London: B.T. Batsford, Ltd., 1985. This covers other textiles as well as household linens.

Hall, Dorothea, ed. *The Gentle Arts*. New York: The Lace Guild, Exeter Books, 1986. Very good for illustrating a variety of categories.

Harbeson, Georgiana Brown. *American Needlework, The History of Decorative Stitchery and Embroidery From the Late 16th to the 20th Century*. New York: Bonanza Books, a Division of Crown Publishers, Inc., 1938. A practical handbook and history covering the various categories during those periods.

Marich, Lilo and Heinz Edgar Kiewe. *Victorian Fancywork*. Chicago: Henry Regnery Co., 1974. Shows many of the patterns used in needlework during the Victorian period.

Montgomery, Florence H. *Textiles in America, 1650–1870*. New York: W.W. Norton, A Winterthur Book, 1984. A well-documented book, as with all Winterthur books. Very necessary for your research.

Swan, Susan Burrows. *Plain and Fancy, American Women and Their Needlework, 1700–1850*. New York: Holt, Rinehart & Winston, 1977. Very well illustrated with the special needlework collection from the Winterthur Museum.

Lace

HISTORY

Lace has been collected for centuries for its fragile beauty, decorative value, and social status. The history of lace spans more than 500 years, and it figures prominently in the areas of social maneuvering and political intrigue for many of those years. In the early days, men, as well as women, were compelled to decorate themselves with lace for social status. They demanded unbelievable yardage of this exquisitely beautiful handmade craft, which in turn required unbelievable hours of labor by many peasant workers. History tells us that Charles I of England required 994 yards of edging for a dozen collars and cuffs, and 600 yards of bobbin lace for his nightwear.

Paintings of the fifteenth through the eighteenth centuries show men of royalty and the wealthy class adorned with lace in many forms, including ruffs at the neck, large cuffs, and even lace falling from the tops of their boots. The women were even more lavishly adorned with yards and yards of lace in all manner of decoration. It was reported that more than 200 people were employed from March to November in 1839 to make the four-yard flounce of Honiton lace for Queen Victoria's wedding gown. (It has been reported that she wore the wedding headdress for many years, especially in the latter years of her widowhood when she dressed only in dark gray and black—just check out the photographs from the late nineteenth century!) Lace remained solely within the province of the upper classes until the advent of lace-making machinery in the early nineteenth century.

The word "lace" is derived from the Latin *laqueus*, meaning a noose or snare. It is easy to understand why it was so designated when we learn the definition of lace. It has been expressed in many terms, but the basic definition is a textile which has been patterned around holes by the manipulation of threads. The threads may be cotton, flax, silk, metallic or other material, whether handmade or machine-made. As a fabric, it must be made of threads, it must have holes to define the pattern, and the threads must have been handled by special movements. It can be referred to as a "lot of holes in air" which have threads worked or twisted around them—ethereal?

We do not know when or where the first systematic looping of threads began, but surely, when early man first designed primitive nooses and snares to catch game, or when he made a simple net to catch fish, the basic technique was born. We are all familiar with the stories of the fishermen of biblical times who cast their nets into the sea. It is difficult to realize that even though thread and fabric go back to pre-historic times, and embroidery and patterned weavings were found in Egyptian tombs, there is little evidence to show that lace existed before the sixteenth century. Some evidence of a form of crochet and net work have been referred to as early as the fourteenth century. It seems that lace was strictly indigenous to Europe, and lace, as we know it, was never mentioned as being developed on any other continent.

The four main types or "families" of lace can be more or less broken down into the centuries in which they were developed: sixteenth century—embroidered laces; seventeenth century—needlepoint laces; eighteenth century—bobbin laces; nineteenth century—machine-made laces, "imitation" laces, chemical laces, and mixed laces. I might also mention that the twentieth century went on to develop the now very popular crazy quilt mix of laces found in household linens and fashion items. This latter type is not a "family" or process, but an ingenious method of utilizing all those fragments and snippets which have been collected from sales or saved from grandmother's trunk. When identifying lace, it is important to be able to place a piece of lace into its proper "family"; the identification process will then become much easier.

EMBROIDERED LACE

Embroidered laces were mostly open work or drawn work in handmade linen using hand-spun linen thread and an ordinary sewing needle. Some of the threads were drawn and/or removed from the fabric's counted spaces, and the remaining threads were then bundled together and sewn in place to create a simple design. The edges of the fabric were loosely whipped in an overhand stitch to prevent fraying. These were usually white. Since this was worked into fabric, it was used mainly as an edging, such as a ruff for collars and cuffs or for altar cloths and vestments. At that time, linen thread was made in short lengths and work from this period will show thick spots where the threads were joined together. This work is still being done today, but with greater finesse by hand and also by machine. Exceptions for today's embroidered laces are that the fabric will be machine-woven, the thread will most often be cotton, and other colors may be used. Early cut work laces were made in northern and southern Europe. Modern-day equivalents are Ayrshire, Broderie Anglaise, and Madeira. Today, handmade cut work is coming in from many countries, with great quantities coming from China.

NEEDLEPOINT LACE

Needlepoint laces are recognized by the buttonhole stitch, which is the basis of all needlepoint lace and makes it immediately recognizable. Such lace is made with a single thread and an ordinary sewing needle. It may appear to resemble embroidery.

Needlepoint, considered by many to be the earliest form of true lace, evolved from cut work where the threads were removed to leave a hole; the edges were worked with a buttonhole stitch and the open center of the space was then filled in with a pattern of closely worked buttonhole stitches to resemble a woven solid. Connecting buttonholed brides connected it to the linen. The two earliest needlepoint laces were *reticella* and *punto in aria*. They both are in the form of geometric squares and circles.

Eventually, needlepoint lace was made by using a pattern drawn on a strip of parchment. Edging threads were tacked down along the design and, by filling in the pattern with row upon row of buttonhole stitch, with linking brides to hold the pattern together, it could then be lifted from the parchment as a lace independent from any base fabric. The designed parchment was then used again to make the desired length.

When we refer to "needlepoint lace" we are *not* referring to what we normally think of as "needlepoint," which is a tapestry. Needlepoint, as an *embroidery* or *tapestry*, is worked on a canvas or linen base with threads and a needle, and it is dependent upon the canvas base to make a complete whole. This type of needlepoint is exemplified in the beautiful pillows, chair upholstery, and many exquisite pieces which the early ladies of this country made for their homes, and today it is also very popular with decorators and home needle workers. Many patterns now come stamped on canvas, as a kit, with the proper threads to complete it, and many are based on antique designs.

There are many laces using the needlepoint method of construction and they answer to many different names, depending on the country or region where they are made. Each area has minor differences, but the use of the buttonhole stitch is still the basic identifying clue. Look for Alencon, Point de France (France); Brussels Point, Duchesse, point and bobbin (Belgium, less point lace was made in Belgium and Flanders than in Italy or France); Florentine, Point de Venise, Gros Point, Rose Point, and Reticella (Italy).

BOBBIN LACE

Bobbin laces are produced by a process of weaving with bobbins, a method by which its name is derived. It is also known as "bone" lace and "pillow" lace. A design is pricked into parchment or cardboard and attached to a pillow; pins are placed in the pricked design to hold the threads as they are woven, plaited, twisted, and formed into a patterned motif which closely resembles woven fabric. The thread is first wound around bobbins and the lacemaker manipulates these around the pins, sometimes using as many as 500 bobbins, depending on the design and width of the lace being made. The width was limited by the width of the pillow before the advent of machine-made lace. As the bobbins hang down from the pillow, their weight serves to keep the threads taut, the design even, and the threads from tangling. "Bone" lace refers to the fact that many of the early bobbins were made of bones from chickens, birds or small animals. These bones were dried and polished, and frequently had a carved design or a sweetheart's name.

Subsequently, bobbins have taken on fanciful designs made from many different materials, with beads and bells on the ends to give them the necessary weight. These bobbins are highly collectible today. There are many laces made by this method, such as: Binche, Bruges, Brussels, Duchesse, and Mechlin (Belgium); Bedfordshire, Buckinghamshire (frequently referred to as "Bucks"), Honiton, and Torchon (England); Chantilly, Cluny, Lille, and Valenciennes or ("Val") (France); Genoa, Plaited, and Milano (Italy).

MACHINE-MADE, CHEMICAL, AND "IMITATION" LACE

The fourth type of lace includes *machine-made laces*, *chemical laces*, and *"imitation" laces*. These date from the nineteenth century, along with the development of many new technologies.

MACHINE-MADE LACE

The era of glorious handmade laces ended with the French Revolution in 1789. Clothing was suddenly very plain, untrimmed except for a meager trim of laces or simple embroidery. Lace was definitely out and most people became puritanical, considering it frivolous and unpatriotic—to say nothing of fearing for their heads! Most collections were destroyed by burning, given to the servants, lost through being stored improperly or cannibalized.

Machine-made lace was a product of the Industrial Revolution. The various machines which produced it were the warp frame, invented in 1775; the bobbin net machine by John Heathcote in 1808; the Pusher machine in 1812; and the Levers machine in 1813. By 1840, machine technology had progressed to producing very good imitations almost indistinguishable from most handmade laces. This was greatly helped by the French invention of the Jacquard "card" system (*see* Jacquard under "Coverlets"). The Great Exhibition of 1851, with fantastic prizes being given by Prince Albert, and the International Exhibition of 1867 had a great influence on the use of machine-made lace and its designs and manufacture.

With the introduction of machine-made laces, the use of lace was no longer the status symbol of the wealthy, as it was soon available to all classes. Women with little money were now able to buy individual lace sprays and motifs each week; they would eventually collect enough to make their own designs by attaching them to machine-made net. Because of the popularity of machine-made lace and the high production rate, it was no longer economical to produce very much handmade lace. As a consequence, the art gradually died out except for the few who clung on to the art. With the advent of the machine, it was now possible to produce lace in wider widths than could be manipulated by hand or on the pillows. This opened up all sorts of design possibilities, not only for fashion but for home decorations as well.

CHEMICAL LACE

Chemical lace was invented by both the Swiss and Germans in 1883 at about the same time. It was derived from machine-made cotton embroidery on silk, after which the silk was then dissolved by the use of chlorine or caustic soda wash. This technique was used to imitate almost all forms of lace, obviously making it much less expensive than the original handmade or machine-made lace. This process was helped by the invention of the Schiffli machine in 1863 by the Swiss and Germans. It produced embroidery on fabric and net by using a continuous thread and a shuttle. Now less drastic processes are used, such as blasting with hot air, making it possible to produce more delicate embroidery that results in a more delicate lace. It is easy to detect chemical lace by the fuzzy appearance to the edges and brides, the lack of definite lace stitches, and a matted appearance to the reverse.

"IMITATION" LACE

During the late Victorian era and the early twentieth century, when women entertained in their homes in the afternoon, there was a fascination with amateur crafts, and this led to the home production of what is termed "imitation" laces. Many of there were not new methods but were based on old processes.

BATTENBERG

Battenberg lace is made from machined braid or tape which is basted down onto a paper or fabric printed pattern, then turned and twisted into curves or angles to follow the outlines. Tapes are then joined by brides and fillings to hold the tapes together. That portion can then be lifted from the pattern and the process continued until the desired length is achieved. The earlier work had a fineness to the brides and fillings that is not evident in recently made battenberg. Look for linen fabric fields in the finer pieces, as well as rings that are plump and well defined and brides that are buttonhole stitched.

One of the most popular early patterns was bunches of grapes made from well-padded rings, the leaves being made from tapes bordering linen doilies, tablecloths, and bedspreads. Frequently these were made from kits. Later, cotton fields were used and the stitching became less artistic, not showing the craftsmanship evident in the earlier pieces.

The market is now flooded with battenberg-trimmed household linens and fashions. The majority is coming from China and is handmade, but does not show the earlier quality of workmanship—and not a "lifesaver" (padded ring) in the lot! Many pieces coming from the Continent are of much finer quality and workmanship. Battenberg is, however, just about the most popular "lace" fashion statement on the market today.

CROCHET

Some form of crochet has been mentioned since the fourteenth century, although it did not become popular as an art form until the nineteenth century when the Irish first produced it in the mid-1840s. It was an important cottage industry during the Potato Famine (1846), when even the men and boys joined women and girls in this endeavor. It is worked with a crochet hook using cotton thread and is identified by the tiered rose petals in the design and the frequent use of the shamrock. Picots are used on the brides, giving it a very lacey appearance. The first lace to be copied by the chemical lace method was Irish crochet, in the 1880s. It is extensively copied in India and China.

In the late 1880–1890s and up through the early twentieth century to about 1940, *filet crochet* was extremely popular. It was worked to resemble needle-run net. The basic pattern was net form, with stitches crocheted in to fill the square holes, creating a pattern. This form was used widely for every conceivable fashion and household item imaginable. In reviewing some of the older trade papers directed to the homemaker—such as *Needlecraft*, dating from 1909—all sorts of patterns were illustrated. These were apparently avidly sought by readers who wrote many letters pleading for more new and exciting patterns. Many booklets of filet crochet designs were published and they, too, are highly collectible today. Flea markets and estate sales are a good source for these.

And, of course, crochet has been designed to imitate many other forms of lace as well. Fancy borders and edgings, inserts, medallions, and all of the various designs for bedspreads and tablecloths have been extremely popular and have kept homemakers busy for years.

KNITTING

Knitting dates from the early 1800s. It is worked with one to four needles and makes horizontal rows of loops from a continuous thread. Knitted lace came into popularity with Victorian ladies who spent much of their leisure time fashioning all sorts of household pieces, as well as clothing. Highly collectible today are the light open-work shawls made of Shetland wool, said to be so fine that one can easily pass a wedding ring through one.

MACRAME

Macrame differs from knotted lace in that it is not made with a needle but by hand. Macrame was used to fringe antimacassars, doilies, and shawls. It is enjoying a revival at present in the form of wall hangings, mats, belts, and all sorts of household and fashion items. Usually, very heavy or coarse threads are used.

TAMBOUR

Tambour, as a lace, is made with a hook and a basic chain stitch on net to create a design. This method is also used on fabric and is considered an embroidery stitch. It is now machine-made, much of it coming from Damascus and other eastern countries. It began commercially in Ireland in 1829 and was referred to as "Limerick" tambour.

TATTING

Tatting dates from the eighteenth century. It fell from grace but was revived at the time of the International Exhibition in 1867. It is made with a shuttle, a continuous thread, and uses one basic knot to secure the loops and picots. It is said that Queen Marie of Rumania was an expert tatter and developed many new techniques. It is used mainly to form edgings, trimmings, collars, cuffs, and other small pieces.

MIXED LACE

Mixed laces are pieces containing different styles of laces in one object, such as a combination of needle and bobbin laces or different laces stitched onto net. Frequently this will include embroidery as well.

CRAZY QUILT LACE

A new use for lace in the past few years is referred to as "crazy quilt." This is not a process or method of construction, but a clever way to use all of those beautiful snippets of lace which we collect and can't possibly discard. All of these differing pieces are stitched onto a lining of fabric and then made into blouses, skirts, pillows, and almost anything the seamstress can devise. One of the most elegant pieces I have seen is a banquet-size tablecloth using hundreds of small pieces and motifs, arranged in a very artful manner, joined by hand and *not* having a fabric underlining. This must have required months of patient planning and sewing to complete. When it comes to lace, you are limited only by the scope of your imagination!

As you delve into the mysteries of lace history, you will find it to be fascinating. Its development has spanned one of the most interesting, intriguing, and explosive periods of our documented history. It is at once a social, political, and industrial history of its time. I highly recommend a further study into the background of lace—this chapter merely skims the surface.

This presentation is by no means intended to be definitive but, hopefully, will assist and encourage you in your enjoyment of lace and your further pursuit into this rewarding hobby. The importance of study and hands-on experience can never be overemphasized. The motto for any collecting is *"research, research, research,"* and *never* trust a "sworn" remark!

COLLECTING TIPS

There are two things to do first before embarking on a shopping trip for lace. Number one: *do your homework*. Although there are many experts in the lace field, not many people in the general public have a working knowledge of this vast subject, so go prepared. Read all you can about it in advance. It is important to have some idea of identification, history, and background of the subject you will be looking for. Number two: *prepare yourself a kit of sleuthing necessities*—a good magnifying glass, measuring tape, a note pad, pen, and a good identification book which, hopefully, you will have read!

Never be shy about asking questions—query the salespersons and get as much information as possible. If you are purchasing for an investment, provenance is equally as important as all other details. Even if you are not investing, the provenance adds interest to your collection.

Examine the article and try to place it in the proper family. Is it a bobbin lace that has woven-appearing toiles? Does it appear to be needlepoint with toiles and brides of buttonhole stitch? Check through the other various categories until you have a feel for its identity. This is where the magnifying glass will be of enormous help. Machine-made lace is almost impossible to identify from handmade lace with the exception that on machine-made lace the designs will all be exactly alike and even; handmade lace will show stitches and designs that are less uniform and some will be tighter or looser in execution and perhaps more random. Until you have learned to spot chemical lace by sight, examine the reverse with the glass—it will seem matted and you will not be able to follow a thread through the design. The edges will appear less smooth and more fuzzy than other lace. Using the glass, check for minor breaks and losses, as well as the type of thread used. Early lace was made from linen or silk. Since the advent of the machine, cotton was used almost exclusively until the twentieth century and the development of man-made fibers. Such examination should help you place any item within its proper time frame. Once done, compare it with the Quality and Condition Keys to assist you in placing it within its proper value scale.

There are many fine shops across the country selling quality laces, but you can still find very good pieces at many flea markets, yard sales, tag sales, and estate sales. Always look for the bag and box lots—this is where you will frequently discover a bargain among the fragments and snippets. Some will be stained, have losses, and be unusable, but the chance of finding one really good piece among the chaff is always possible.

You will not see very much handmade lace on the market today. Machine-made lace dates from 1830, and since that time until the present it has been, and still is, made in great quantities. The finer and older machine-made lace is highly collectible, lovely, and just as desirable (and certainly more affordable) than early handmade lace, if and when you find it. As discussed in the "Introduction," many early and fine handmade collections were destroyed or allowed to slip into disrepair. Because of the labor and time involved, lace of that quality will never be made again in any quantity. Many groups around the country are now meeting and learning the old techniques, but I doubt that few modern women will be able to spend the weeks required just to make a few inches of their favorite lace, and certainly not for the market!

I understand that the finest machine-made lace today comes from France. I, personally, know of an Italian family of lacemakers in New Jersey who designs all of their own patterns and has their machines built and programmed in France. It is certainly fascinating to watch the machines in operation.

See the listing of museums at the end of this section and pay a visit whenever you are in the vicinity of one. It is important that you see and appreciate the really beautiful and elegant handmade pieces which are now housed and preserved in these fine institutions.

QUALITY AND CONDITION KEYS

CONDITION KEYS

Measures only the physical condition of the article and not the quality of design, material or workmanship.

Fine Condition (FC): Complete and original or restored to original condition; retains its original ground; without stains, fading or losses. Most desired condition for collecting.

Good Condition (GC): Restored or replaced ground, nearly to original as possible. No breaks, fading or stains. May need cleaning.

Average Condition (AC): Needs minor mending; may have weak spots; some losses; minor stains and fading; needs cleaning. This is most often the condition in which lace is found.

Poor Condition (PC): Most often found in fragments or removed from an article; frequently will show weak spots, stains, and fading; needs cleaning. Collectible for doll clothes, crazy quilt, and other small articles where the good sections can be utilized with other fabrics. Usually found in box lots at flea markets and estate sales. Often a bargain, but not for investment!

QUALITY KEYS

Measures the stylishness and collectibility of the piece within its category.

Good Quality (GQ): Exhibits standard characteristics of the piece, whether handmade or machine-made.

Very Good Quality (VGQ): More desirable example because of above average design, materials, and workmanship.

Superior Quality (SQ): Exhibits every known feature found for such items, handmade or machine-made, with design, material, and workmanship of highest quality. Most desirable for collecting.

GLOSSARY OF TERMS AND TYPES OF LACE

The subject of lace is highly specialized and involved, using many unfamiliar terms relating to laces from many countries. For this reason, I felt it would be helpful to have a glossary of terms and types of lace right up front before the listing of items to assist in quick identification of the various categories and word usage. These terms relate mainly to lace and probably may not be needed for any other category in this book. If there are any terms included in the listings not shown in this glossary, check with the general "Glossary" at the back of the book. Although I have tried to show all of the terms and specialized references which may be useful, we may not all be perfect! In such a case, please check the "Bibliography" at the end of this section and pay a visit to your local library or the nearest museum.

Alencon. French needlepoint, named for the city of Alencon. Design is usually floral and has a thick cordonnet surrounding the toile. The ground is usually on an ordinary net. Considered a "winter lace" because of the thickness. Now referred to as "bridal lace" because of its popularity with brides. Approximate time of origin is 1665.

Battenberg. A lace made by forming tapes into designs which are held in place by brides. Battenberg has become a generic term for most tape lace in the United States today. It is a form of Renaissance lace very popular in this country for tea cloth edgings in the early 1900s. The original used handmade tapes; now almost all are machine-made. (*See also* "Imitation Lace" under "History" of lace)

Binche. Belgium, seventeenth and eighteenth centuries. A fine, usually straight-edge lace, similar to Valenciennes. Identifying characteristic is five-sided or star-shaped mesh ground, often having scattered spots like snow.

Bobbin. A weaving process which takes its name from the mechanics used—bobbins, usually of wood or bone, worked on a pillow. The toiles appear to be woven fabric. Also known as bone or pillow lace. (*See also* "Bobbin Lace" under "History" of lace)

Bone. Term used to refer to bobbin lace because the early bobbins were made of bones from small animals, birds or chickens. Same as bobbin.

Bridal Lace. Originally a lace made from blue thread and worn by wedding guests rather than by the bride herself in Elizabethan times. Today it refers to Alencon and Chantilly, which is most often used for bridal gowns.

Brides. The leg or strut threads which hold the toiles together in the pattern. Also called bars, legs, and ties. Most frequently used term is "brides."

Brussels. Belgium lace. Refers to a variety of laces produced in various parts of Belgium, including bobbin, needlepoint, and mixed. In recent years, a decorated net is often referred to as Brussels.

Bucks. England, eighteenth and nineteenth centuries. This is an abbreviation for Buckinghamshire lace. Originally a bobbin lace; it usually has a simple ground and a silky cordonnet around the toile. Frequently has flowers or fruits in design and many different filling stitches in the spaces. Mayflower and honeycomb are commonly used.

Buttonhole Stitch. The basic stitch of all needlepoint lace. Same as the half-hitch knot in rope tying. Examine the buttonhole edging on your clothing. Very similar stitches have been found in relics dating from the Bronze Age (ca. 2,000 B.C.) in Denmark.

Carrickmacross. Ireland. Named for the city of the same name. It is an appliqué of sheer muslin over the pattern in the lace and the edges are whipped into place over the toile. It is considered a mixed lace. Dates from about 1820.

Chantilly. Named for the city in France. First made in 1740. A bobbin lace, it was originally made in black using flax and silk. Uses a simple net ground with floral designs, swags, and ribbons. Has a slight cordonnet around the toiles. Today it is popular for bridal gowns and is machine-made from rayon or nylon fibers in many colors. Narrow widths are often referred to as baby lace.

Chemical Lace. Process is discussed under "History" of lace.

Cluny Lace. A bobbin lace that originated in France in the early nineteenth century. It is a heavy-plaited lace of geometric design, often with radiating wheat ears (long, narrow lozenge forms). It is usually heavy and made of linen or cotton, and is often used in furnishings rather than fashion. Cluny takes its name from an ancient house in Paris which is now the Musee Cluny.

Cordonnet. A heavy or raised outline thread around the motif or toile to make it more sharply defined.

Crochet. Discussed under "Imitation Lace" in "History" of lace.

Darned Lace. Also known as darned net. One of the earliest forms of lace work. Made with a needle in running or darning stitch on a knotted ground, as in filet, or on machine-made net to form a design pattern. Most popular all over Italy in the sixteenth century.

Duchesse. Belgium, nineteenth century. Bobbin lace. Usually associated with Brussels, though sometimes Bruges. This lace was bolder in pattern and used heavier thread, which made it faster to make than other laces of the time. Identified by clusters of flowers similar to forget-me-nots and with ribbed leaves. Sometimes it has small inset motifs of needlepoint lace.

Embroidered Lace. See under "History" of lace.

Embroidered Net. Nets made by machine, then decorated by hand- or machine-embroidery. One popular form is tambour, which is made with a small needle using the chain stitch. When worked on fabric it is considered an embroidery; when worked on net it is considered an "imitation" lace. (*See also* "Imitation Lace" under "History" of lace)

English Lace. This was never considered in the same high regard as laces made on the continent. However, the major lace machines were invented in England and the Industrial Revolution originated in England, so their machine-made laces were very important in the nineteenth century. English lace curtains are now enjoying renewed popularity with Victorian-style decorators and owners of old Victorian houses.

Filet. Popular in many countries for centuries. Derived from the French *filet* for safety net or drag net. The filet refers to the knotted mesh on which the pattern is worked. Machine-made mesh does not have knots in the corners of the square holes. Patterns for filet work were published in Venice as early as 1532. Copies of these designs in crochet were very popular in the United States in the 1920s. (*See also* "Imitation Lace" under "History" of lace)

Flounce. A wide strip of lace with a border on one edge; the other edge to be gathered or pleated and attached to clothing, usually skirts or sleeves.

Galloon. A length of lace having scallops on both sides.

Gimp. Has several meanings, but generally refers to the thick thread that is used in bobbin lace to edge the outline of the toile or design in the lace (except Binche and Valenciennes). The thread is formed with a core of parchment or a heavy cord. Similar in use to cordonnet, except thicker and more prominent.

Gros Point. Bold form of Venetian needlepoint, originating about 1620. Identified by bold flowers with heavily padded borders. The padding was made with bundled flax or wool thread which had been buttonholed over. This process gave the finished lace a heavy, carved, shiny appearance, and due to the color of the flax it resembled carved ivory. The finer pieces have spreading flowers closely touching without the use of many brides.

Ground. The background of the lace which holds the designs together or on which the designs are attached.

Guipure. Can be either bobbin or needlepoint, with designs or toiles held together by brides and not having a net or patterned ground.

Hairpin Crochet. A form of lacy crochet worked on a hairpin-shaped instrument or a two-pronged fork with a crochet hook. It is very narrow and used as an edging, frequently on handkerchiefs or baby clothes.

Honiton Lace. Name derived from a town in East Devon, England. Dates from early nineteenth century and used on Queen Victoria's wedding gown. It is a bobbin tape lace applied to net ground. Early Honiton used toiles made separately and then applied to net and held in place with brides. It is very similar to Brussels lace.

Illusion. A silk net that is almost invisible. Made on a bobbinet machine at Lyons in 1828; now in a plain, slightly stiffened form ("tulle illusion"). It was revived in the 1940s and specially made for the royal wedding outfits. It was used as bridal veils for the weddings of Queen Elizabeth II (1947), Princess Anne (1973), and the Princess of Wales (1981). It is said to appear like a "shimmering mist around the head and shoulders." (*See also* Tulle)

Imitation Laces. See under "History" of lace.

Insertion. Strip of lace having both edges straight. Intended to be placed between two sides of fabric or lace, joining them into one independent whole.

Irish Crochet. See "Imitation Lace" under "History" of lace.

Lappet. Long narrow streamers of lace attached to the back of the head and falling below the shoulders. A requirement for appearance in court from about 1660 to the nineteenth century. Now used as a decorative tie at the neck.

Legs. Same as brides, bars, and ties.

Macrame. Spanish-Moorish origin. (*See also* "Imitation Lace" under "History" of lace)

Mesh. A single unit of net which has each hole surrounded by thread the entire network of the ground.

Mixed Lace. Made of mixed techniques, such as a combination of both bobbin and needlepoint on net. Often this has embroidery included.

Needlerun Lace. An embroidery on net made with a running stitch.

Net. A mesh ground made by machine rather than by hand.

Picots. Tiny pearl-like loops on the edge of lace.

Pillow Lace. Used to describe bobbin lace since it is worked on a pillow. However, there are some needlepoint and knotted laces that are worked on a pillow as well. Check other identifying methods to determine which lace you are studying. Term is most frequently used for bobbin lace.

Point. An abbreviation for needlepoint.

Punto in Aria. Italian meaning "stitches in air." Identified as an embroidered lace worked in buttonhole stitch. (*See also* "Needlepoint Lace" under "History" of lace)

Renaissance Lace. Lace which has the design outlined in purchased tapes. Also known as Branscombe, Battenberg, Princess, and Sardinian Point. (*See also* "Battenberg" under "History" of lace)

Reseau. A ground of small meshes filling the open spaces of a lace. Same as ground.

Reticella. Italian for "little net." (*See also* "Needlepoint Lace" under "History" of lace)

Rose Point Lace. Italy, seventeenth century. A Venetian needlepoint lace. The flowers are smaller and the cordonnets less raised, but the flowers are tiered and the brides more elaborate than in gros point.

Schiffli. See "Chemical Lace" under "History" of lace.

Snails, Slugs. Little shapeless forms sometimes seen in the ground of Honitan lace. Thought to have been made by children.

Sprig. An individual motif or fragment, usually not all made by the same person, used to form a lace by being appliquéd to net and held together by brides. The lace thus formed is sometimes referred to as sprig lace.

Tambour. See "Imitation Lace" under "History" of lace.

Tatting. See "Imitation Lace" under "History" of lace.

Tenerefe Lace. Canary Islands origin. Made of cotton on a four-sided or round frame having fifty-two pins around the rim. The pins hold the threads while various patterns and forms are worked using a needle. Most designs are circular. The pins are then removed to free the finished lace.

Toile. French for linen or cloth. General use today refers to the denser part of the lace—such as the pattern, trails, and filings—as opposed to the ground in both bobbin and needlepoint lace.

Torchon. French for duster or rag. A strong bobbin lace made originally from heavy flax thread. Because it was quick and cheap to make by hand, it was referred to as Beggar's Lace. Usually made in a geometric pattern showing fanlike shapes and with a scalloped edge. Since the early twentieth century it has been perfectly copied by machine, now using cotton thread. More often used for household decorations than for clothing.

Tulle. French. A net made by machine, usually silk.

Valenciennes Lace. Belgium, seventeenth and eighteenth centuries. Named for a lace-making town on the French-Flemish border. It is a bobbin lace with a light filmy design. It is identified by a row of minute pricked holes surrounding the toiles. It usually shows flowers and flowing fronds. There are no cordonnets. It has always been expensive to make because of the time required to complete. It is still comparatively expensive, although machine-made, because of the fine thread used. In recent years, 90% cotton and 10% nylon have been used to prevent breakage during manufacture. Often used in christening gowns; the narrow "Val" is frequently referred to as baby lace.

MARKET TRENDS

For many years lace was out of fashion, but now, considered an art form, it is making a dramatic comeback. Since the late 1970s up through the 1980s there has been a considerable upsurge in the market. Interest among collectors has not been at such an all-time high since the early days when the royalty and gentry vied with each other for the most lavish use of lace. Many workshops have been formed around this country and in Europe to research and teach the early techniques of handmade lace.

Lace appeals to the artistic sense and to the love of the beautiful in all of us. It also appeals to our appreciation for history and for the many years of painstaking work which went into the development of lace. It is not surprising that in this age of nostalgia, therefore, the excitement of decorating lies in a method which is, on the one hand, totally individual, yet also reaches back to the historic, as well. We are using lace for clothing fashions as never before in this century, and also for home decoration. Every fashion magazine or advertisement shows clothing with some touch of lace, not only in adult fashions but for children and babies as well. We still feel a great love for the christening gowns which have been made with yards and yards of lace trim and we still hold on to these family traditions. Many young women today want handmade Victorian wedding gowns with all of the white work and lace frothings.

Home decorators use lace in household fashions because it is compatible with quilts, coverlets, antique linens, and the wonderful reproduction fabrics on the market today. Is there any wonder that lace is currently a big market?

This nostalgia will be with us for some time to come, as will the market for laces of all kinds. Hopefully, we will be able to preserve them for the generations down the line, for we will never again be able to replace what we have been entrusted with at the present time.

CARING FOR
YOUR LACE

Machine-made lace is much more sturdy than we realize, and yes, it can be laundered. First of all, test to see if it has dry spots. This is done by holding it in two hands, with slack between, near the ear. Very gently stretch the lace; if it makes minute cracking sounds then it is too dry, brittle or fragile to launder. If it is not dry and does not have any thin areas or broken threads, it will do well if placed in a net lingerie laundry bag and placed in the washing machine on delicate cycle; use tepid water and mild soap. It must be rinsed several times to remove all residue of soap. To dry, pat it out onto turkish towels and gently urge it into original shape; allow to dry flat without being disturbed. Blot up excess water with a household sponge—never wring or twist.

If it appears to be delicate, float it in a pan of water large enough for it to be totally surrounded by water; let it soak. Do not pick up by edges but slowly let water flow out and add rinse water, still keeping the lace afloat. To dry, just pick up the entire mass together and gently pat out onto a turkish towel, using the sponge, and very carefully pat it to the original shape and allow it to dry in that position. Use a very gentle laundry agent, such as Orvus WA paste, a nondetergent cleaner. Use one teaspoon to a gallon of tepid water, soak about forty-five minutes, and then rinse and dry as above. Oxalic acid (be careful—poisonous—use no metal) and sodium perborate are good on tough stains and rust, and Era is very good for blood and other protein stains. Be careful with black lace—the dye usually runs.

To press, lay the lace face down on a towel on a padded board. The iron will then be touching the reverse side. The heat setting should be lower than specified for the material.

If you have a piece of heirloom lace that is too fragile for use and which you wish to keep, baste it to a piece of muslin for protection from stress.

Proper storage is very important. *Never* store in plastic bags! Plastic will retain moisture and allow the lace to mildew and deteriorate. The best method is the use of acid-free tissue and boxes. These are readily available through mail order, if not locally (see below). Always place tissue between single layers of lace and place in boxes or in well-laundered old sheets and pillow cases. Do not fold because the edge of the creases will, in time, become brittle and fall apart or will show age stain. If the item is too large to fit in a box without folding, layer in thick paddings of tissue and roll gently Boy Scout fashion. This method of rolling is also good if storing in old sheets or pillow cases because there will not be any folded creases to be weighted down. Even temperature and humidity must be maintained—never store in the attic or near a heating unit. If the temperature is comfortable for you, it will do just fine for the lace. If kept stored, lace should be removed and aired at least twice a year and rerolled in different directions. *Remember*—lace, as well as all textiles, is singularly sensitive to the effects of light, heat, moisture, insects, and dirt.

Never use drastic measures. When working with handmade lace, heirlooms or very fragile pieces, defer to professional conservationists and trust their expertise if you have any doubts. Just contact your nearest museum and they will point you in the proper direction. We owe it to future generations to preserve whatever we can of what has been passed on to us. Too much has been lost in the past.

For acid-free storage boxes and tissue, you may contact the following:

University Products, Inc.
P.O. Box 101
Holyoke, MA 01041-0101
Phone: (413) 532-3372 or (413) 532-9431

Talas
104 Fifth Avenue
New York, NY 10010

DISPLAYING AND USING YOUR LACE

Be creative with your lace! Fashion decrees the use of lace on many outfits of clothing at present. The collars and cuffs which you have collected may be tacked onto necks and sleeves with running stitches or stitch velcro on the edges for easy removal. Lappets and crocheted edging from pillow cases are being used as neckwear with blouses, dresses, and simple sweaters. Many items of clothing and household decorations are being made from pieces of lace put together in a crazy quilt manner. This is an excellent way to use pieces which are too small to be used alone, or pieces salvageable from larger fragments. Cut your pattern first from thin fabric, stitch the lace down in a pleasing arrangement, then sew the seams together. The fabric underlining will give the lace the needed protection from stress and retain the shape of the article being made. Lace applied over a pastel color base is stunning. A lace doily makes a very pretty bodice for a little girl's dress—just add fabric for the skirt. My brothers, sister, and I were christened in a gorgeous gown, forty-five inches long, which had been fashioned from our grandmother's Victorian white lace wedding dress. It was complete with a petticoat of batiste over a petticoat of flannel and lace without end. It saw a great deal of loving service through the years and finally disintegrated completely—going with many tender memories.

Collected edgings applied to large napkins are especially attractive—the edgings need not match nor be white. Dress a festive dining table or a champagne table at a reception with a collection of lace curtain panels arranged to the floor over an undercloth. Here, again, they need not match—lace just melds together beautifully. A lace tablecloth that is too fragile to be used frequently makes a glamorous canopy for the bed, and strew the bed with pillows covered in collected bits of lace. Lace scarves look right at home being used as valances at the window—just toss them over the rod and pin in swags at the corners. Be sure to use stainless steel pins to prevent rusting and keep the lace high enough to be out of the sun. The list is endless!

There are many attractive ways to display lace as wall hangings. Bobbin lace motifs of animals and children can be framed individually on colored backings and placed in a grouping as you would with silhouettes. Grandmother's wedding handkerchief, framed and hanging over the head of your bed, could bring sentimental memories. Any piece of beautiful lace can be used to make a wall hanging for any room, no matter what period or style the decor. Lace blends perfectly into period rooms and also makes a statement with contemporary ones. Recently, I saw large lace pieces which had been sandwiched between clear Plexiglas. These were hung with transparent threads from the ceiling and used as room dividers. They were very striking; the lace appeared to float in space. The owners had several pieces and so were able to rotate them to prevent too much strong light, as well as cut down on the time spent with an overzealous heating system.

Although there are many ways to display framed pieces, there is a strong warning before you frame and glass-over any lace that is old or valuable. You *must* have the lace processed by experts because of the specific needs of antique textiles. All textiles must be surrounded by acid-free components or they will eventually discolor and disintegrate. There are so many elements to consider that it is most important to have a preservationist prepare all textiles for framing if they are old or valuable, or if they are important to you as a family inheritance or for sentimental reasons.

LACE LISTING

The items listed in this lace section will be shown according to the family category. By placing each group together in this manner it should be easier to locate the particular article which you may be interested in. First, read the description for each category, then examine the article and turn to the proper heading for that item.

Many items below will be made of linen, cotton or other fibers as the central part of the article. However, if the most important or predominant area of the article is the lace adorning it, or if it is all-over lace, it will be listed here under the proper family of that lace. If the fabric is the most important area of the article, without any lace trim or any major lace trim, then it will be listed under "Linens."

EMBROIDERED LACE INCLUDING CUT WORK AND DRAWN WORK

Banquet Cloth 72″ × 144″ Drawn and cut Ca. 1935 Italy
Ivory linen; border of cut and drawn floral designs attached by brides; deep-pointed edges; the entire center is of drawn work in ¼″ square filets. All needlework done in brown thread. With twelve matching napkins, 24″ × 24″. *(See photo 22)* SQ/FC *$1,800 Set (D)* .... $900–$1,800

> Notice the spiderlike arrangement of brides which hold the motifs in the open cut work (see photo); this is typical of early work of this type.

Bridge Cloth 52″ × 52″ Drawn work Ca. 1920 China
Silk pongee; natural color; wide hem is hemstitched; design has been worked from threads remaining after planned warp and weft threads have been removed. All handmade. *(See photo 23)* VGQ/FC *$85 (D)* .... $45–$85
Doily 18″ × 24″ oval Cut work Ca. 1930–1940 Madeira
White linen with pale blue embroidery edges; needlepoint brides and toiles in cut spaces; filet lace edging. *(See photo 24)* GQ/AC *$15 (D)* .... $12–$35
Luncheon Cloth 54″ × 60″ Cut work Ca. 1920–1930 Madeira
White linen; cut designs with brides; floral embroidery; scalloped edges. An exquisitely made cloth. *(See photo 25)* SQ/FC *$375 (D)* .... $295–$450
Napkins, Cocktail 9″ × 9″ Drawn work Ca. 1940 Madeira
Ivory-colored linen; beige threads; drawn design in multifilet motif. VGQ/AC *$30 Set of six* .... $18–$45
Napkins, Dinner 26″ × 26″ Cut work Ca. 1940 Italy
Natural linen; open cut area in one corner filled in with floral needlepoint toile, 2″ × 3″; surrounded by embroidery. Natural needlepoint lace edging, 1″ wide. Machine-made lace applied by hand. VGQ/FC (Unused) *$195 Set of twelve (D)* .... $125–$225
Tablecloth 68″ × 102″ Cut work 1920–1930 Italy
Natural-colored linen; needlepoint lace toile inserts and machine embroidery; machine-hemstitched border. *(See photo 26)* GQ/FC *$125 (D)* .... $75–$150

PHOTO 22

PHOTO 23

PHOTO 24

PHOTO 25

PHOTO 26

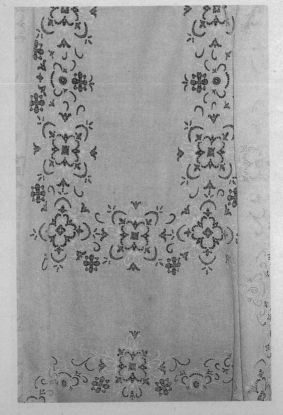

PHOTO 27

Tablecloth 68″ × 84″ Cut work Ca. 1935 Madeira
White linen; insets of floral design in white needlepoint lace toiles; pale blue
edging and embroidery; center motif in rectangle form of same design; border
of white filet lace 2″ wide. Eight napkins with corner motif and filet lace edging,
20″ × 20″. GQ/AC *$195 Set (D)*... $165–$225
Table Runner 44″ × 18″ Cut work 1910–1930 Madeira
White linen; cut work filled with machine-made needlepoint lace toiles; edged
in machine-made filet lace. Thin areas. *(See photo 27)* GQ/AC *$18 (D)*.........
.... $25–$65
Table Runner 18″ × 54″ Drawn Work Ca. 1920 China
White linen; all hand-work. *(See photo 28)* GQ/AC *$18.50 (D)*........ $15–$45

The CONDITION KEY measures only the physical condition of the article and
not the quality of design, material or workmanship.
Fine Condition (FC): Complete and original or restored to original condition; retains its original ground; without stains, fading or losses. Most desired
condition for collecting.
Good Condition (GC): Restored or replaced ground, nearly to original as
possible. No breaks, fading or stains. May need cleaning.
Average Condition (AC): Needs minor mending; may have weak spots; some
losses; minor stains and fading; needs cleaning. This is most often the condition in which lace is found.
Poor Condition (PC): Most often found in fragments or removed from an
article; frequently will show weak spots, stains, and fading; needs cleaning.
Collectible for doll clothes, crazy quilt, and other small articles where the
good sections can be utilized with other fabrics. Usually found in box lots at
flea markets and estate sales. Often a bargain, but not for investment.

PHOTO 28

PHOTO 29

PHOTO 30

The QUALITY KEY measures the stylishness and collectibility of the piece within its category.

Good Quality (GQ): Exhibits standard characteristics of the piece, whether handmade or machine-made.

Very Good Quality (VGQ): More desirable example because of above average design, materials, and workmanship.

Superior Quality (SQ): Exhibits every known feature found for such items, handmade or machine-made, with design, material, and workmanship of highest quality. Most desirable for collecting.

Table Runner 18″ × 60″ Drawn work Ca. 1930 Italy
White linen; in a classical design of peacocks and flower vases; filet background, all hand-drawn and stitched. Designs on both ends. *(See photo 29)* VGQ/GC *$95 (D)*... $45–$125
Tea Cloth 56″ × 56″ Drawn work Ca. 1900 Italy
White linen; all designs are drawn and whipped by hand. A fine example. *(See photo 30) SQ/FC $125 (D)* .... $50–$135
Tea Cloth 54″ × 54″ Drawn work Ca. 1920 Italy
White linen; all designs are drawn and whipped by hand. Another fine example. *(See photo 31) SQ/FC $120 (D)* .... $45–$135

This type of cloth, in various sizes, was very popular before World War II. You will find many new ones on the market at present, but they will be made of cotton having a lot of sizing. They will not have the quality of fabric and workmanship as the originals. Now coming from China as well as the Philippines.

Tea Cloth 56″ × 56″ Cut and drawn work Ca. 1935 Philippines
White linen; "Army-Navy" type having alternating squares of cut and drawn work with floral filet insertions on linen and squares of floral design filet lace; 2″ filet lace border. No losses. VGQ/AC *$95 (D)*...................... $65–$125

PHOTO 31

PHOTO 32

NEEDLEPOINT LACE

Border 54″ × 64″ × 4″ wide Gros point Ca. 1900 Italy
Ecru, border removed from worn linen tablecloth. Outer border with a center strip; special attention to corners. Machine-made toiles, hand-assembled. No losses. (A bargain from an estate sale.) *(See photo 32)* VGQ/AC *$25 (ES)* .....
.... $15–$50

Doilies (2) 18″ dia. and 24″ dia. Rose point Ca. 1900 Italy
Ivory color; all-over rose design; scalloped edges; machine-made; no losses; two minor breaks which may be tacked. VGQ/AC *$95 Pair (D)* .... $50–$125

Doily 26″ dia. Gros point trim Ca. 1900–1910 Italy
Ecru with linen center, 12″ dia.; floral design; machine-made, hand-assembled, and hand-applied to the linen center. VGQ/FC *$125 (D)* .... $50–$150

Fragments (3) 6″ × 18″, 12″ × 14″, and 2″ × 36″ Gros point Ca. 1900 Italy
All ecru; typical floral patterns. GQ/AC *$45 Lot (ES)* .... $15–$50

Napkins, Dinner 26″ × 26″ Point de Venise trim Ca. 1900 Italy
Set of twelve; ecru linen with large motif with putti and flower in one corner; 1½″ matching lace border. Machine-made lace, hand-assembled and hand-applied to linen. Very elegant. SQ/FC *$550 (ES)* .... $450–$600

Pillow Cover, Boudoir 12″ dia. Rose point Ca. 1930 Italy
Made from fragment, ivory colored, underlined with pale blue satin; narrow edging of point lace; button back cover. GQ/AC *$75 (D)* .... $35–$125

Place Mats 11″ × 15½″ Alencon Ca. 1935 France
Set of eight, luncheon size; ivory color; machine-made; all-over floral pattern; scalloped edges. With eight napkins, 14½″ × 14½″; edged in narrow matching lace. GQ/AC *$75 (D)* .... $50–$95

Place Mats 11½″ × 18″ Point de Venise Ca. 1930 Italy
Set of eight with a runner, 18″ × 42″; ecru; machine-made, hand-assembled; design of flowers and swirls. Minor stains on one place mat. Without napkins. No losses. VGQ/AC *$195 Set (D)* .... $150–$300

PHOTO 33

Scarf 16″ × 32″ Gros point Ca. 1900 Italy
White; machine-made, hand-assembled. Three quatrefoils with flower motifs; border with flowers and moths; scalloped edges. *(See photo 33)* VGQ/AC *$65 (D)*.. $50–$95

Scarf 17″ × 45″ Alencon Ca. 1930–1935 France
Ecru, all-over floral design; machine-made. *(See photo 34)* GQ/FC *$23 (D)*... .... $18.50–$25

Tablecloth, Banquet 84″ × 144″ Point de Venise Ca. 1940 China
Ecru-colored cotton thread; all-over design of leaves and medallions surrounded by borders of flowers. Hand-assembled. Few stains, no losses. With set of twelve napkins of ecru linen with a corner motif and 1″ matching lace on edges. The quality of the lace was superior to the workmanship of the napkin construction. The lace was machine-applied to the raw edge of fabric, 24″ × 24″. Napkins unused, paper labels still attached. *(See photo 35)* GQ/AC *$750 Set (ES)* .... $500–$2,500

Vanity Set Center, 12″ × 18″; Two side pieces, each 9″ × 12″ Gros point Ca. 1930 Italy
Ivory color; putti and floral design; machine-made. GQ/AC *$45 (D)*............ .... $25–$65

BOBBIN LACE

Bridal Veil 48″ × 80″ Brussels Ca. 1940 Belgium
White, scrolling border (8″ deep) on net field. Some breaks in net field. Machine-made. *(See photo 36)* VGQ/AC *$235 (D)*................................ $150–$250

Cap Adult size Valenciennes Ca. 1850 France
Ivory color; very fine threads; hand-sewn. *(See photo 37)* GQ/GC *$25 (ES)* ... . $15–$50

PHOTO 34

PHOTO 35

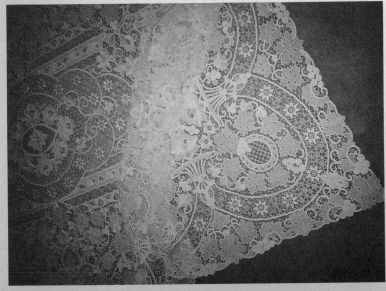

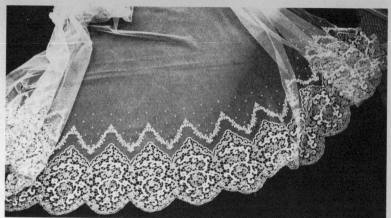

PHOTO 36

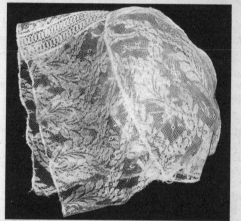

PHOTO 37

PHOTO 38

Cape 45″ dia. Chantilly Ca. 1890–1920 France
Black, complete circle; showing typical floral, ribbon, and swag pattern. No losses or breaks. *(See photo 38)* VGQ/GC *$225 (D)* .... $150–$250
Cloth 32″ dia. Cluny Ca. 1900–1920 United States
Ivory color; machine-made lace hand-applied to linen center. Slight fold-line stain; will launder. (Probably made from a kit.) *(See photo 39)* GQ/GC *$50 (D)*... $25–$75
Collar, Bertha 6″ × 24″ Brussels Ca. 1900 Probably United States
Ivory color; machine-made; fine, lightweight. *(See photo 40)* VGQ/FC *$125 (D)*... $75–$175
Collar-Cuff Set Collar, 5″ × 54″ Brussels Ca. 1880 Belgium
Ivory color; very fine cotton thread; collar has extended tie; with matching cuffs. Machine-made, hand-assembled. Minor age discoloration. *(See photo 41)* SQ/FC *$125 Set (ES)*... $75–$150
Doilies 12″ × 16″ oval Bobbin Ca. 1920 France
Pair, ivory color; center motif in form of lady with a basket of fruit. Machine-made toiles attached to edging by handmade plaited brides. VGQ/GC *$95 Pair (D)*... $75–$125
Doily 14″ dia. Cluny 1987 Finland
Ecru-color linen center; handmade lace edging, hand-applied in very fine stitches. Mint condition. *(See photo 42)* SQ/FC *$25 (D)*........................... $15–$35

My niece purchased this from the factory in Finland after watching the lacemaker complete it. Apparently lacemakers are still plying their trade—even if it is for tourists!

The CONDITION KEY measures only the physical condition of the article and not the quality of design, material or workmanship.
Fine Condition (FC): Complete and original or restored to original condition; retains its original ground; without stains, fading or losses. Most desired condition for collecting.
Good Condition (GC): Restored or replaced ground, nearly to original as possible. No breaks, fading or stains. May need cleaning.
Average Condition (AC): Needs minor mending; may have weak spots; some losses; minor stains and fading; needs cleaning. This is most often the condition in which lace is found.
Poor Condition (PC): Most often found in fragments or removed from an article; frequently will show weak spots, stains, and fading; needs cleaning. Collectible for doll clothes, crazy quilt, and other small articles where the good sections can be utilized with other fabrics. Usually found in box lots at flea markets and estate sales. Often a bargain, but not for investment.

The QUALITY KEY measures the stylishness and collectibility of the piece within its category.
Good Quality (GQ): Exhibits standard characteristics of the piece, whether handmade or machine-made.
Very Good Quality (VGQ): More desirable example because of above average design, materials, and workmanship.
Superior Quality (SQ): Exhibits every known feature found for such items, handmade or machine-made, with design, material, and workmanship of highest quality. Most desirable for collecting.

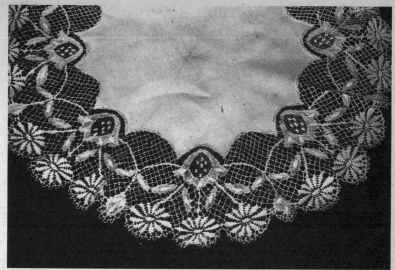

PHOTO 39

PHOTO 40

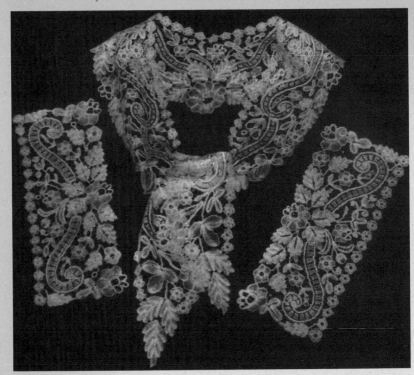

PHOTO 41

PHOTO 42

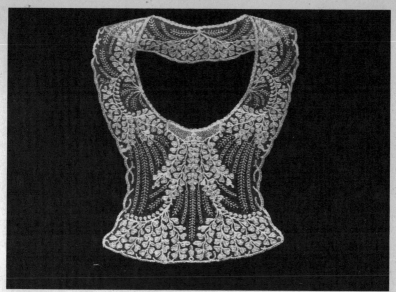

PHOTO 43

Dress Trim 14″ × 12″ Buckinghamshire Ca. 1900 England
Ivory-color cotton thread; neck trim and frontal combined; machine-made. Typical Bucks design. *(See photo 43)* GQ/AC *$18 (ES)* .... $12–$45
Flounce 5″ × 72″ Lille Ca. 1900 France
Ivory color; machine-made. Lille is often very similar to Bucks. Few minor breaks in net. *(See photo 44)* GQ/AC *$15 (ES)*........................... $10–$35
Galloon 6″ × 54″ Valenciennes Ca. 1880–1890 France
Natural color; floral toiles; scalloped both edges. Machine-made of very fine cotton thread. *(See photo 45)* VGQ/GC *$25 (D)* .... $10–$45
Handkerchief 14″ × 14″ Honiton Ca. 1920 England
Ivory color, very fine linen with 1½″ machine-made lace, hand-applied. *(See photo 46, left)* GQ/AC *$18 (D)*... $10–$25
Handkerchief 12″ × 12″ Honiton Ca. 1920 England
Ivory color, very fine linen with 1″ machine-made lace, hand-applied. *(See photo 46, right)* GQ/AC *$15 (D)* .... $10–$25
Handkerchief 14½″ × 14½″ Valenciennes Ca. 1870 France
White; very fine batiste with 2¼″ machine-made "Val" lace border. Provenance: wedding of Annie Herman, eastern Pennsylvania. *(See photo 47)* GQ/AC *$20 (D)* .... $10–$35
Lappet 6″ × 45″ Brussels Ca. 1850–1870 Belgium
Cream color, extremely fragile, fine, and lightweight. Appears to be handmade, although pieces of this quality were machine-made at this time. Shows flowers, leaves, and scrolls. *(See photo 48)* SQ/FC *$195 (D)* ....$95–$225
Motifs R., 4″ × 6″; L. 5″ × 8″ oval Bobbin Ca. 1920 France
Natural color. Machine-made toile and edge tape, handmade brides. Still attached to mesh backing. *(See photo 49)* GQ/GC *$5 Each (ES)* ....$2–$15

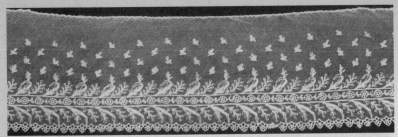

PHOTO 44

PHOTO 45

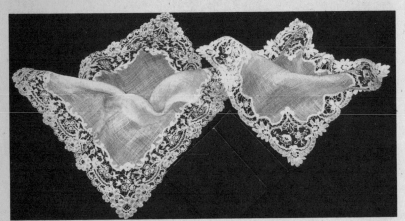

PHOTO 46A   PHOTO 46B

PHOTO 47

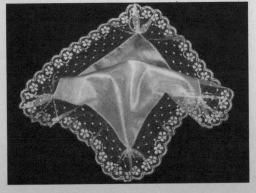

PHOTO 48

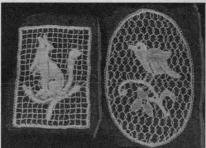

PHOTO 49

PHOTO 50

PHOTO 51

PHOTO 52

Motifs   R. and L., 6″ × 6″; Center 8″ dia.   Bobbin   Ca. 1920   France
Natural color, machine-made toiles and edge tape, handmade brides. *(See photo 50)* GQ/GC   *R. and L. $5; Center $8 (ES)* ....$2–$15

> The insert motifs shown here make especially attractive wall hangings when
> backed by colored fabric and framed. This type of bobbin lace is made on a
> cookie pillow—so called because it is round and flat; when placed on a spin-
> dle it facilitates rotation while the lace is being worked.

Pillow Cover   18″ × 34″   Chantilly   Ca. 1910–1920   France
Cream-color lace with inserts of embroidered batiste, all machine-made and hand-
assembled. Lined and backed with peach-colored iridescent taffeta. Label reads:
"Made in France." *(See photo 51)* SQ/FC   *$225 (D)*...................$150–$275
Tablecloth   72″ dia.   Cluny   Ca. 1880–1890   France
White linen edged and inset with machine-made Cluny lace. The outside border
is 12½″ deep, center insert is 8″ deep. Hand-assembled. This elegant cloth has
a few breaks which can be easily retacked. No losses. This was a bargain! *(See
photo 52)* VGQ/AC   *$75 (ES)* ....$75–$225

MACHINE-MADE, CHEMICAL, AND "IMITATION" LACE

MACHINE-MADE LACE

The majority of laces on the market today are machine-made. The glorious handmade laces of the eighteenth and early nineteenth centuries
are almost all in museums and private collections and out of reach of the

average collector. There are shops specializing in the elegant pieces—and the prices match the rarity! There have been a few lots offered in auction house sales in the past few years from estates which are now being liquidated. So, it *is* possible to collect handmade laces if you are lucky enough to inherit them or if you have the opportunity to shop in major cities where they are available to specialty shops and auction houses.

The majority of the laces listed in the previous three sections are machine-made unless otherwise designated.

CHEMICAL LACE

Bodice Medium size Chemical Ca. 1920–1930 United States
White; lace front and collar on a net bodice to be worn under a dress or blouse. Collar is fully ruffled. Side ties at waist. *(See photo 53)* GQ/AC *$25 (D)*.......
.... $15–$50
Collar-Cuff Set Small Chemical Ca. 1920–1930 United States
White cotton; all-over floral design; bias tape binding for attaching to clothing. GQ/AC *$7.50 Set (D)* .... $5–$15
Cuff Chemical Ca. 1940 United States
One of a pair. White cotton; very attractive design and a good example of this type lace. *(See photo 54)* VGQ/GC *$3.50 Pair (ES)*........................ $2–$10

PHOTO 53

PHOTO 54

PHOTO 55

PHOTO 56

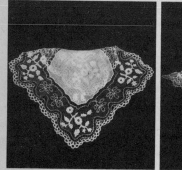

PHOTO 56A   PHOTO 57

PHOTO 58

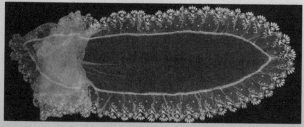

Doily 24″ dia. Chemical Ca. 1940 United States
White cotton; overall pattern of flowers, leaves, and swirls. GQ/GC *$4 (ES)*..
.... $2–$15

Galloon 5″ × 60″ Chemical Ca. 1930–1940 United States
White cotton; floral and leafy swag. Good example. *(See photo 55)* VGQ/GC *$5 (D)*.. $3–$15

Galloon 4″ × 48″ Chemical Ca. 1930–1940 United States
White cotton; floral center, scalloped edges. Both ends finished. *(See photo 56)* GQ/GC *$3.50 (D)*... $2–$15

Handkerchief 10″ × 10″ Chemical Ca. 1950 United States
White cotton lace on batiste center. Machine-attached. *(See photo 56A)* GQ/AC *$3.00 (D)*.. $1.50–$10

Handkerchief 12″ × 12″ Chemical Ca. 1920 Japan
Cream-colored cotton lace on peach-colored weighted silk. Example to show how old weighted silk will spilt in the fold creases when not stored properly. *(See photo 57) No value*..

Lappet 6″ × 48″ Chemical Ca. 1880 England
White cotton net with 2″ ruffled lace edging. *(See photo 58)* GQ/GC *$15 (ES)* .... $10–$35

Vanity Set Center, 12″ × 16″; two sides, 10″ × 12″ Ca. 1930 United States
Ivory-colored cotton; all-over pattern of round motifs; edges scalloped. GQ/GC *$10 Set (D)*.. $5–$15

"IMITATION" LACE

BATTENBERG

Curtain Panels Each 36″ × 84″ Battenberg Ca. 1900–1910 United States
All white; linen panel with one side and bottom of 12″-wide floral, leaf, and swirl-pattern tape lace. Well-formed design. Pocket heading. Minor restorations. GQ/GC *$145 Pair (D)*... $50–$175

Doily 27″ dia. Battenberg Ca. 1880–1890 United States
All white; fine linen center; very well-defined bunches of grapes with well-padded rings; leaves are of very narrow tapes and fine threads; spaces filled with spider web-like brides. Hand-sewn to center. This is a very fine example. *(See photo 59)* SQ/FC *$135 (D)*.. $50–$150

PHOTO 59

PHOTO 60

Doily 32″ dia. Battenberg Ca. 1895–1900 United States
All white; small scalloped center of linen; wide swirling pattern; handmade and
applied to linen. *(See photo 60)* SQ/FC *$85 (D)* .... $50–$95
Luncheon Cloth 54″ × 60″ Battenberg Ca. 1880–1890 United States
All white; linen center with leaf and swirl design; well-defined rings. Handmade
and hand-applied to linen. *(See photo 61)* VGQ/GC *$95 (D)* .... $50–$125
Scarf 18″ × 44″ Battenberg Ca. 1920 United States
All white; designs of daisylike flowers and leaves with circular corner motifs.
Needs minor tacking. No losses. *(See photo 62)* GQ/AC *$35 (D)* ..... $25–$50
Tablecloth 68″ × 84″ Battenberg Ca. 1930 United States
All-white linen; rectangular center motif and outer edges of floral, leaf, and vine
pattern. Needs minor tacking. No losses. GQ/AC *$75 (ES)* .... $50–$150
Tea Cloth 54″ × 54″ Battenberg Ca. 1890–1900 United States
All white; linen center with border insertions and lavish edging in floral and leaf
pattern. Needs minor tacking. No losses. *(See photo 63)* VGQ/AC *$95 (D)*....
.... $75–$150

PHOTO 61

PHOTO 62

PHOTO 63

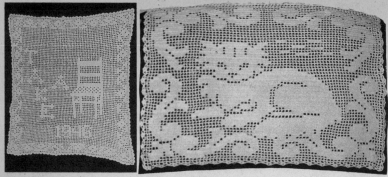

PHOTO 64   PHOTO 65

CROCHET

Antimacassar 15″ × 18″ Filet crochet Ca. 1946 United States
White; showing a chair and "Take a (chair) 1946." Arm pieces are simple with
same border design. *(See photo 64)* GQ/GC *$42.50 Set (D)*............ $25–$50
Antimacassar 12″ × 15″ Filet crochet Ca. 1910 United States
Cream color; design has cat encircled in scrolls. Three pieces including back
and two arm covers. *(See photo 65)* VGQ/GC *$45 Set (D)* .... $25–$65
Antimacassar 14″ × 18″ Filet crochet Ca. 1910 United States
Cream color; shield shape, with center of "kissing parrots" surrounded by roses.
Three pieces—center and two arm covers. *(See photo 66)* VGQ/GC *$65 Set
(D)*.. $35–$75

> Antimacassars make very attractive pillow covers when lined with fabric of
> your color choice.

Bedspread 88″ × 104″ Crochet Ca. 1930 United States
Cream-color cotton thread; hexagonal shape, six-point star shapes and shield
motifs; 6″ hand-tied fringe on three sides. *(See photo 67)* GQ/AC *$285 (D)* ..
.... $195–$375

PHOTO 66

PHOTO 67

PHOTO 68

Bedspread 72″ × 104″ Filet crochet Ca. 1890 United States
All white; center medallion oval insert, 18″ × 24″, showing putti gathering fruit from tree. Three sides with deep-pointed design; crochet in each ''v.'' Fine quality linen in two panels expertly hand-joined at center. This spread would make an elegant and unusual canopy or a beautiful table dressing with a pastel-color undercloth. This was a bargain purchased at an estate sale! *(See photo 68)*
SQ/AC *$95 (ES)*..$95–$350

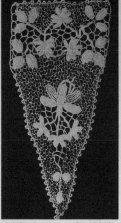

PHOTO 69

Bodice Insert 6″ × 12″   Irish crochet Ca. 1910–1920 Ireland
White mercerized cotton, fine thread. Handmade with picots on brides; heavy toiles with double raised leaves. *(See photo 69)* GQ/AC *$12.50 (ES)* .... $10–$25
Bread Tray Cover 24″ × 24″ overall Crochet Ca. 1920–1930 United States
White; linen center; flaps are in triangular shape with round medallion motifs. *(See photo 70)* GQ/GC *$25 (D)* .... $20–$35
Bread Tray Covers Assorted Crochet Ca. 1920–1930 United States
White; examples of various patterns done in filet crochet. *(See photo 71)* GQ/ GC *$7.50–$15 Average (D)* .... $5–$25

The CONDITION KEY measures only the physical condition of the article and not the quality of design, material or workmanship.
Fine Condition (FC): Complete and original or restored to original condition; retains its original ground; without stains, fading or losses. Most desired condition for collecting.
Good Condition (GC): Restored or replaced ground, nearly to original as possible. No breaks, fading or stains. May need cleaning.
Average Condition (AC): Needs minor mending; may have weak spots; some losses; minor stains and fading; needs cleaning. This is most often the condition in which lace is found.
Poor Condition (PC): Most often found in fragments or removed from an article; frequently will show weak spots, stains, and fading; needs cleaning. Collectible for doll clothes, crazy quilt, and other small articles where the good sections can be utilized with other fabrics. Usually found in box lots at flea markets and estate sales. Often a bargain, but not for investment.

The QUALITY KEY measures the stylishness and collectibility of the piece within its category.
Good Quality (GQ): Exhibits standard characteristics of the piece, whether handmade or machine-made.
Very Good Quality (VGQ): More desirable example because of above average design, materials, and workmanship.
Superior Quality (SQ): Exhibits every known feature found for such items, handmade or machine-made, with design, material, and workmanship of highest quality. Most desirable for collecting.

PHOTO 70   PHOTO 71

Doily 24″ × 24″ Filet crochet Ca. 1890–1900 United States
White; quatrefoil form; formed filet crochet with roses. *(See photo 72)* SQ/
FC *$85 (D)*.. $50–$95
Edgings Assorted Filet Crochet Ca. 1890–1930 United States
White cotton thread; assorted patterns of handmade filet crochet. Each removed
from worn pillow cases. These are examples of lot bargains available at various
sales, found along with items which may be a total loss! Use for pillow cases,
towel edgings, little girl's skirt trim, collar and cuff sets—the list is endless. *(See
photo 73)* GQ/GC *$3 Lot (ES)*...............:................................... $1–$15
Napkin Envelope 12″ × 24″ Filet crochet Ca. 1890–1910 United States
White; filet crochet envelope with rose motif and monogram. *(See photo 74)*
VGQ/GC *$18 (D)* .... $10–$35
Scarf 18″ × 54″ Filet crochet Ca. 1980–1990 United States
Ivory mercerized thread. Scene showing Neptune and "merpersons" frolicking.
Edged in scallop design. Needs minor racking. No losses. Good example of
design for framing. *(See photo 75)* GQ/AC *$25 (ES)* .... $15–$75

PHOTO 72

PHOTO 73   PHOTO 74

PHOTO 75

PHOTO 76

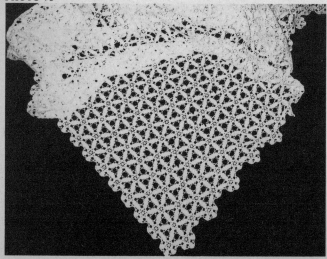

PHOTO 77

PHOTO 78

Tablecloth 54" × 65" Crochet Ca. 1940 United States
Cream color; 2" dia. hexagonal motifs, hand-assembled. Minor tacking needing. No losses. *(See photo 76)* GQ/GC *$45 (D)*............................. $35–$75
Tea Tray Cover 18" × 24" Filet crochet Ca. 1935 United States
White; showing tea accessories and "Take a Cup For Auld Lang Syne." Four linen napkins with teapot motif in one corner. *(See photo 77)* GQ/GC *$35 Set (D)*.. $25–$50
Window Valances 40" × 42" Filet crochet Ca. 1920 United States
White; motifs of eight-pointed stars and mesh, handmade tassels. *(See photo 78)* VGQ/AC *$110 Pair (D)* .... $75–$150

KNITTED LACE

Bedspread 85" × 106" Knitted Ca. 1920–1930 United States
Ivory color, mercerized cotton thread, 6" geometric squares in assorted pattern samples. Crocheted edging four sides plus 6" hand-tied fringe on three sides. VGQ/FC *$375 (D)* .... $250–$425
Doily 12" dia. Knitted Ca. 1910–1920 United States
White, fine mercerized cotton thread; floral and spoke pattern; scalloped edging. Would be lovely backed with fabric and framed. GQ/AC *$15 (ES)*...... $5–$25
Gown Yoke 4"-width lace Knitted Ca. 1900–1910 United States
White. Knitted in a lacy pattern with square neck and sleeve bands attached. Removed from worn fabric. GQ/GC *$15 (ES)*................................$5–$35
Pillow Cover 14" dia. Knitted Ca. 1950 United States
Natural color cotton thread; knitted in a pinwheel pattern with scalloped edging. Underlined and backed with fabric to match. Button back. VGQ/AC *$18 (ES)* .... $10–$45

PHOTO 79

MACRAME

Tablecloth 32″ × 48″ Macrame Ca. 1920 United States
Off-white, heavy linen; drawn work on each end; macrame in pointed form on each end with small handmade tassels on ends and scattered along sides. For a library table. *(See photo 79)* GQ/AC *$25 (D)* .... $15–$45

TAMBOUR

Curtain Panels 36″ × 90″ Tambour Ca. 1935 United States
Ivory color; machine-made; all-over floral, leaf, and spray design on net; scalloped edges on three sides; pocket top. Some losses of design. *(See photo 80)* GQ/AC *$65 Pair (ES)*...$50–$250
Tablecloth 64″ × 86″ Tambour Ca. 1920 France
White; machine-made; floral and spray design on net with elegant cartouche in center. Losses to design and minor tears in net. *(See photo 81)* GQ/PC *$25 (ES)* ....$25–$250

> Condition is very important. The two tambour pieces shown suffer in value from losses. Tambour is worked in a chain stitch which will unravel like a knitted sweater if care isn't taken to tie down any stray thread immediately.

TATTED LACE

Handkerchief 12″ × 12″ Tatted Ca. 1950 United States
White linen center with hemstitched edge with 1″ tatted lace attached, ruffled; ombre shades of lavender. VGQ/FC *$10 (D)* ....$5–$35

PHOTO 80

PHOTO 81

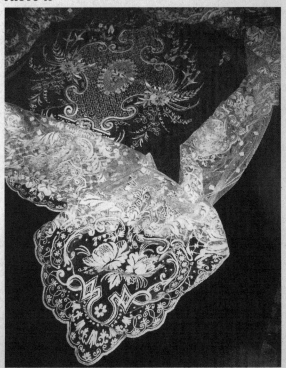

Handkerchief, Wedding 13″ × 13″ Tatted Ca. 1985 United States
All white; 8″ × 8″ fine linen center with wide, ruffled, tatted border. Hand-embroidered flowers in each corner. Fortunately, this work is still being done. SQ/FC *$65 (D)* .... $15–$75

Lace Edging 1″ × 72″ Tatted Ca. 1940 United States
White; lovely lacy pattern suitable for baby clothes or lingerie. Another bargain find! VGQ/FC *$5 (ES)* .... $2–$15

MIXED LACE

Collar 6″-width lace Mixed lace Ca. 1880–1890 France
Ivory color; mixed laces of bobbin toiles and very narrow picoted silk tape. Machine-made components, hand-assembled. A very elegant collar. *(See photo 82)* SQ/FC *$175 (D)* .... $65–$225

Collar 3″-width lace Mixed lace Ca. 1930 Ireland
Ivory color; main portion of collar is Carrickmacross lace (appliqué) mixed with Chantilly at front tabs and edging. The cut work is filled with a variety of brides. Machine-made. *(See photo 83)* GQ/GC *$18 (ES)* .... $12–$35

PHOTO 82

PHOTO 83

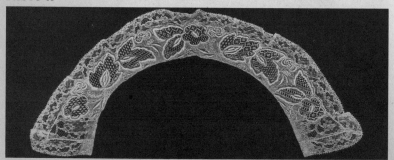

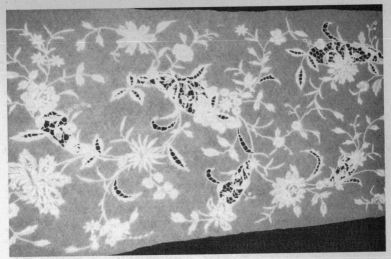

PHOTO 84

PHOTO 85

Table Runner 20″ × 144″ Ca. 1885–1900 France
Ivory color; machine-made net, inserts of needlepoint and bobbin toiles. Hand-embroidered floral designs. Edges unfinished. *(See photo 84)* SQ/FC *$275 (D)*
.... $150–$300

Tea Cloth 42″ dia. Mixed lace Ca. 1900–1910 Italy
All white; center is fine quality linen; inner insert is needlepoint; outer border is exquisitely worked in bobbin lace figures in reliefs, attached by brides to needlepoint floral and leaf toiles with a scalloped edge of bobbin lace. A truly fine example of very high quality. *(See photo 85)* SQ/FC *$325 (D)* .... $250–$350

CRAZY QUILT LACE

As mentioned before, "crazy quilt" is not a method or process, but a collection of wonderful snippets of all sorts of laces which have been collected with the intent to utilize—and save forever. They are worked together in whatever arrangement the individual is happy with. Most often these pieces are backed with a thin piece of fabric to stabilize the fragile lace, then stitched together just as our grandmothers did with their precious pieces of silks and velvets, seen in those wonderful Victorian crazy quilts, that are now so highly collectible.

Blouse   Size 8/10   Mixed laces of many ages   United States
Ivory color; a collection of at least seven kinds of laces stitched together into a very attractive lady's blouse in a Victorian style. This blouse was put together on a net base to help support and stabilize the fragile lace; cuffs have ribbons run through and tied in a bow at the wrist. *(See photo 86)* SQ/FC   *$285 (D)*...
.... $150–$450

These beautiful fashion items are now hot on the market, and the sale prices depend on types of laces, individual workmanship, and acceptable styles. Check carefully for fragile or thin areas—you would not want your blouse to lose a sleeve halfway through the first wearing!

Handkerchief   12″ × 12″   Crazy quilt   Ca. 1900   United States
White; voile center on diagonal; mixed laces of Chantilly, Val, and chemical. *(See photo 87)* GQ/GC   *$7.50 (D)*...$5–$15
Tablecloth, Banquet   84″ × 144″   Crazy quilt   Ca. 1940   United States
Off-white; a variety of laces and strips of 2″-wide net ruching assembled into a very exciting banquet cloth. No underlining; all laces are hand-assembled onto each other, having a center medallion; swags of the ruching; other laces filling in spaces and a medallion of Brussels lace in each of the corners. (Unfortunately, this was sold while I was examining it, and I was unable to photograph it even though I was camera-ready. The new owner was immediately very skeptical!) VGQ/FC   *$1,200 (D)* .... $500–$1,500

PHOTO 87

PHOTO 86

MUSEUMS AND CLUBS

MUSEUMS

Cleveland Museum of Art
11150 East Boulevard
Cleveland, OH 44106

Cooper-Hewitt Museum of Design
Smithsonian Institution
Fifth Avenue at 91st Street
New York, NY 10018

Metropolitan Museum of Art
Fifth Avenue at 82nd Street
New York, NY 10028

National Museum of History and Technology
Smithsonian Institution
Washington, DC 20560

The Valentine Museum
1015 East Clay Street
Richmond, VA 23219

CLUBS

Lace Guild of New York
P.O. Box 1249, Gracie Street Station
New York, NY 10028
Presents periodic lectures and workshops.
Many members are involved with old
lace in a professional capacity.

BIBLIOGRAPHY

Bath, Virginia Churchill. *Lace*. Chicago: Henry Regnery Co., 1974. This book not only outlines background history, but shows diagrams of techniques and many photographs of categories, up to modern textiles. Hardcover.

Dolan, Maryanne. *Old Lace & Linens, Including Crochet: An Identification and Value Guide*. Florence, AL: Books Americana, Inc., 1989. Paperback.

Earnshaw, Pat. *The Identification of Lace*. Second edition. Aylesbury, Bucks, UK: Shire Publications, Ltd., reprint 1989. I have found all of the Earnshaw books to be most helpful. Paperback.

——. *A Dictionary of Lace*. Second Edition. Aylesbury, Bucks, UK: Shire Publications, Inc., 1984. Paperback.

Henneberg, Alfred F.A. von. *The Art and Craft of Old Lace*. Berlin: Ernest Wasmuth, 1931. Excellent for stitch diagrams and techniques. Hardcover.

Kraatz, Anne. *Lace, History and Fashion*. New York: E.P. Dutton, 1988. Hardcover.

Palliser, Bury, Mrs. (1805–1878). *History of Lace*. London: Constable and Low, 1875. New York: Dover. Dover edition, first published in 1984, is an unabridged republication of the edition published by Charles Scribner's Sons, New York, 1911. This work is amazing in scope and scholarship since Mrs. Palliser had no earlier body of work to refer to and did all of the research on her own. In the 1901 edition, some areas were rewritten to take into consideration modern research which might have shown any faulty information. *History of Lace* is still considered a standard on which much modern work is based. It is a must for your library if you have any interest in lace. Paperback.

Warnick, Kathleen and Shirley Nilsson. *Legacy of Lace: Identifying, Collecting and Preserving American Lace*. New York: Crown Publishers, 1988.

Quilts

HISTORY

Interest in American quilts is now at an all-time high. The proliferation of quilt societies and clubs is staggering; museums are having special quilt exhibitions; and antiques shows are awash with quilts of every hue imaginable, of all patterns and periods. Newsstands are flooded with quilt magazines of all types, and every decorator magazine has its share devoted to the display and use of quilts, not only in the home, but in business establishments and institutions as well. This new appreciation of the quilt and of the time-consuming efforts of the early homemaker has raised the quilt from a household necessity and craft to an art form.

The quilting of textiles for warmth and beauty has been with us for centuries. Early quilts were mentioned in Egyptian writings going back hundreds of years, which is not surprising since they excelled at the manufacture of cotton, linen, and wool at an early date. There are several references to quilts in the Bible. The early Chinese used quilted robes to wear for protection from the cold. One of London's street peddlars, "Mrs. Diggs of Thread Needle Street," who sold notions from her basket, was considered well off because she had three quilted silk petticoats. Old French records reveal a quilt for Marie Antoinette. It was made by her mother's court ladies, required eight years to complete, and was appliquéd and embroidered with hearts and flowers and other love motifs. Quilts have not always been as fine as this!

By the early eighteenth century in this country, quilting had become a social event, even in Boston among the wealthier classes. For the less wealthy folk, quilting bees meant special times for getting together. Women would gather at a home where there was room enough to put up a quilting frame and would work on quilting by day; the men, in from the fields, would then join the women for a hearty supper spread followed by dancing. This was also an official way of announcing a young woman's engagement. The woman was expected to have made a number of quilt tops by the time of her engagement, which would then be quilted in time for the wedding. The quilting bee was also one way for women to help each other in time of need and loneliness.

On the long trek westward, the quilt was an important part of the cargo. When the travellers had settled, there would be little time for quilt making until the land had been cleared, shelter built, and the crops in. A woman was expected to work beside her husband in all of these labors and still keep her family fed and clothed. After the trials of moving westward, quilt patterns achieved new names as women were influenced by their new surroundings, but many of the traditional patterns were cherished and passed on to their daughters and friends.

There developed an interesting tradition among the Appalachian quilt makers. They lived in remote areas and did not have access to many new pieces of fabrics; they worked mainly with scraps and worn-out clothing. Many women who required a large number of quilts, but could not find the time to make "everyday" quilts, would take new fabrics and the necessary thread to these mountain women in the fall. These women would then piece the quilt tops for them while wintering over in their cabins. When spring came, the tops would be collected and delivered to a woman who specialized in quilting; she would then complete the quilts. This was referred to as "pieced on half." The quilt-top maker was allowed to keep half of the fabric and thread furnished as her pay, which allowed her to make her own supply with new fabric. The mountain woman took much pride in her ability to design and piece these tops, and was left free to choose whatever pattern she felt was suitable for the fabric. These Appalachian quilts are highly sought after today.

LINSEY-WOOLSEY

When the settlers first came to these shores from England, they brought quilts with them. Linsey-woolsey quilts had been made in England for some time, and they were most likely the type of quilts that came with the settlers. They also were probably the first quilts to be made in the New World. The name is derived from the process of weaving linen as the warp thread and wool as the weft; it also is named for the village of Linsey in Sussex, England, where this type of quilt was first made. The solid fabric was underlined, stuffed, and quilted, making a warm, sturdy, long-lasting bedcover. When the land was cleared and planting begun, flax was among the first crops to be planted along with food. The homemaker depended on linen and tow, made from flax, for clothing as well as household furnishings, and it was equally as important as food. Textiles coming from England were expensive and arriving shipments were few and far between.

Linsey-woolsey was made on narrow looms and a quilt top could be in two and sometimes three parts. It was a heavy stiff fabric and the beautiful stitching seen on some is a miracle considering the difficulty of stitching through the three layers. Homemade vegetable dyes were used which produced some lovely shades, especially the turkey reds and indigo blues which were highly desired because they blended so well with crewel-work bed hangings. Sometimes the later linsey-woolsey was glazed by rubbing the surface with stones or by using beaten egg whites. The sheen resembles the shiny worn seat of old blue serge trousers!

A WALK THROUGH A SOUTHERN MUSEUM

The color section of this book is devoted to the Valentine Museum in Richmond, Virginia. This fine, small house museum opened to the public in 1898, the gift of Mann S. Valentine II, a chemist, manufacturer, and art patron. He gave his home and collections to the people of the city of Richmond along with an endowment to create this excellent museum. Today the Valentine collects, preserves, and interprets materials related to the life and history of the city, within the context of American urban and social history. The museum holds these materials for research and reflection, creating new knowledge through research and communicating these findings through exhibitions, publications, and programs.

In 1812, on a lovely, tree-lined street in what was then a very fashionable area of downtown Richmond, the Wickham family moved into their new home. They were considered wealthy at the time and had such neighbors as Chief Justice John Marshall, whose home is across the street. The block had many lovely homes and the residents enjoyed a social life as befitted the times. The Wickhams had a large and lively family, complete with many slaves, horses, and stables. When the family finally dispersed, Mann S. Valentine II purchased the home. The Wickham-Valentine House, a National Historic Landmark, is considered one of the nation's finest examples of neoclassical architecture and design. A restored formal garden behind the house is open to the public, as is the studio of E. V. Valentine, brother of the museum's founder and a noted sculptor of many famous Civil War figures.

The museum now consists of four connected nineteenth-century facades, whose original residents had been neighbors of the Wickhams and the Valentines, and is nearly one block long. The integrity of these facades has been maintained while utilizing the combined expanded interior space for the museum's extended collections.

The collections of the Valentine Museum constitute the most comprehensive body of primary source material for interpreting the life and history of Richmond—its modest beginnings as a riverbank trading post, its swift rise to become the twelfth largest city in the industrial nation by the turn of the nineteenth century, its international role as capital of the Confederacy, and the twentieth-century evolution of its industrial, commercial, political, and cultural institutions.

The museum's nationally recognized textile and costume collection, the largest in the South, is among the best in the United States, with more than 20,000 costumes, 10,000 accessories, and 10,000 flat textiles, of which 5,000 pieces are lace. The museum also displays quilts, coverlets, and samplers.

As you enter the front door, you will see renovation in progress, starting with the front door itself. The facade had become Victorianized during the late nineteenth century. Fortunately, the original door and surround was still behind the new facing and is now being uncovered to expose the original 1812 structure. Among the most notable features of this impressive project are spectacular wall paintings, the most complete set of their kind extant in the United States. They are being uncovered and will appear as they were originally. The museum houses many collections of many differing interests, but since we are focusing on flat textiles, we will visit that area of interest in this book.

The collection begins with an infant's christening cap and dress dating to 1668, and some laces and embroideries of the late seventeenth century. A large group of late nineteenth-century household textiles of all kinds contributes information useful in decorating homes of that period. Photo 1 shows a pillow cover of cut work and darned net with inserts of bobbin lace and is from the nineteenth century. We see a beautiful ca. 1860 handkerchief with drawn work and embroidered motif of the Milan Cathedral, edged with Valenciennes lace in photo 2. Next, in photo 3, a towel shows intricate hand-embroidery in bright colors, monogrammed and with hand-knotted fringe, ca. 1800. In the lace collection we found the next three pieces to be especially lovely and representing a breadth of interest: photo 4 is a fan leaf in Brussels lace; photo 5 shows a detail of a piece of Point de Gaz flounce; and photo 6 is a section of Binche lace, Flemish bobbin, ca. 1700–1750.

Their quilt collection is the largest and most varied in the state and is being added to constantly. The next four photographs are but a small area of the collection, but show diverse styles and periods. First, photo 7 is a portrait crazy quilt with a likeness of Robert E. Lee in the center, made in 1884; all of the pieces are silk and in excellent condition. Photo 8 is an early appliquéd quilt made with motifs snipped from imported chintz and additions of embroidery on a white ground, very finely quilted by hand and known as Broderie Perse. The next, photo 9, is a great example of a log cabin pieced and appliquéd quilt, with figures and a fancy embroidered border, made in 1920. The final, photo 10, is a charming child's "ABC" quilt, made in 1877 by Matilda E. S. Smith of Richmond. The next three photographs are various coverlets from the early nineteenth century and show just a sample of the collection. Photos 11 and 12 are double weave and made by two documented weavers, P. H. Anshutz and David Haring (this one woven for Leah Naugle, Dec., 1833). Photo 13 is a detail of a jacquard coverlet showing one of the charming motifs found in many coverlets of that period and widely copied in silhouettes and embroidery.

Needlework is represented in the next six photographs. Photo 14 is a piece of Berlin work done in beads (in progress), ca. 1870; photo 15 is a detail of a cornucopia from a larger embroidery; photo 16 shows a detail of a sixteenth-century Italian embroidery showing very intricate work of that period. Photo 17 is of an extremely unusual miniature sampler only $1\frac{1}{2}'' \times 1\frac{1}{2}''$ square, made by Judith Smith of Richmond, Virginia, in 1780. Next is a darning sampler worked in 1765 (photo 18); and last, a wonderful collection of needlework pieces gathered together in a collage representing a variety of construction methods (photo 19).

These samples should whet your appetite for a trip to the charming southern city of Richmond, Virginia, and a leisurely visit through the Valentine Museum. You will experience southern hospitality at its fullest from trained docents who give tours several times a day, and after your tour, take a stroll through the well-designed garden behind the museum. During the months from April to October, enjoy a boxed lunch, available from the museum, while enjoying the garden visit.

As with all museums, these collections shown are not always on view. Check ahead for a schedule of what is being featured. The staff of the museum will make their facilities available for research if an appointment is requested in advance.

1. A pillow cover from the nineteenth century of cut work and darned net, with inserts of bobbin lace.

2. This handkerchief, ca. 1860, shows the art of very fine drawn work and is embellished with embroidery. Valenciennes lace is the edging.

3. The towel shown here is a fine example of colorful embroidery and hand-knotted fringe, which was popular at the turn of the eighteenth century.

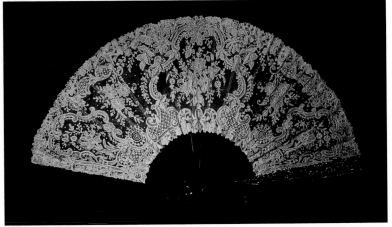

4. Brussels lace was used extensively for fans. This leaf is an exquisite example.

5. A detail of a section of Point de Gaz lace flounce.

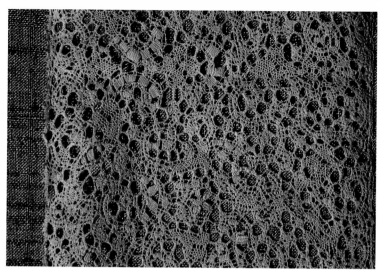

6. This is a section of a very fine Binche lace (Flemish bobbin lace), ca. 1700–1750.

7. Robert E. Lee is featured in this extremely fine example of a crazy quilt, all silk, dated 1884.

8. *A very early Broderie Perse quilt made from chintz motifs stitched onto a white ground and artistically quilted.*

9. *An unusual combination of the log cabin design mixed with silhouettes, with a fancy, embroidered border.*

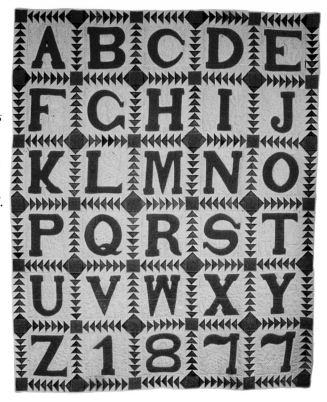

10. A child's quilt made in 1877 by a Richmond resident, Matilda E. S. Smith.

11. This shows an example of a double-weave coverlet made by a documented weaver.

12. *David Haring made this double-weave coverlet for Leah Naugle in December 1833.*

13. *The motif in this detail of a jacquard coverlet is charming and has been copied extensively in silhouettes and embroidery.*

14. *Berlin work in progress, using beads in the design.*

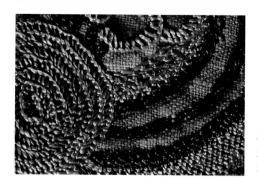

15. *Detail from a large embroidery showing the intricate work involved in this cornucopia.*

16. *This Italian embroidery dates from the sixteenth century.*

17. *A very rare and exquisite miniature sampler, shown here full size (inset). It is dated 1780.*

18. A darning sampler worked in 1765.

19. This is a collage of various needlework pieces found in the collections at the Valentine Museum.

These glazed covers, referred to as "calimanco," were finer than the early linsey-woolsey and were already popular by the early eighteenth century. Some can still be seen in museums, colonial museum houses, and occasionally on the market. Unfortunately, no quilts of the sixteenth century have survived in America.

PATCHWORK

It is difficult to research which came first in America, the appliquéd or the pieced quilt, since no seventeenth-century examples have survived. After the first few hard years of settling an unknown land, women must have yearned for something more decorative than the solid-color linsey-woolsey quilts and turned to their work baskets for scraps and worn-out clothing to piece together fresh quilt tops. Could appliquéing, in this country, have grown out of the patch-on-patch used to preserve clothing by suggesting a more artistic and interesting use for those scraps? The busy homemaker was soon turning out attractive "patchwork" quilts, which included both pieced and appliquéd. By the early eighteenth century, England had developed quilt making into a high level of artistry. The thrifty homemakers in America were determined to express themselves too, so the art of making patchwork quilts became a devotion. Apparently these were developed in England and America at about the same time, independent of each other. By the beginning of the eighteenth century, American women were turning out quilts of beauty and sophistication.

The oldest documented American quilt was made by the ancestors of the Honorable Leverett Saltonstall of Massachusetts, in 1704. It was made of silks and brocade in an all-over pattern of small squares pieced with triangles. The paper used as backing for these tiny triangles had been cut from the Harvard College catalog of 1701. It has a border of handmade woolen ball fringe on three sides.

Women started giving names to their quilts suggested by the events in their lives and the young nation. Soon they were trading patterns with family and friends. Sometimes the given names followed the pattern, but frequently the pattern names were changed as they travelled across the country and the maker experienced new challenges and events. Many patterns across the country may be practically identical but have entirely different names.

The most basic patterns for pieced quilts are the "four-patch" and the "nine-patch." The four-patch is a square made from four pieces of equal size that, when stitched together, make a perfect square. The "nine-patch" square is composed of nine blocks of equal size making the square. By differing the arrangement, color, and fabric within the square, many different patterns are achieved. Some of the blocks may be made with triangles forming the block, but the square will always contain the basic four or nine blocks. There are hundreds of pattern names using the four-patch and nine-patch as the basic arrangement. Some may have sashes dividing the squares and some may have single, double, and triple borders, lending originality to those quilts based on the four-patch and the nine-patch. They are simple, easy to make, and work up quickly. The finished product is limited only by the imagination of the quilt maker.

WHITE WORK

White work is another whole cloth quilt. It originated in Europe in the sixteenth century and was popular in this country from about 1790 to 1820. The fine white fabric was woven in two or three strips on narrow looms and had a backing of coarser linen. These rarely had a center stuffing and were used as spreads. Being of a solid color, the quilter had leeway to be artistic and creative with the design for an all-over stitched pattern. These represented many hours of painstaking stitching, since this was the major focus of the quilt. When the tiny stitches were tightly done the design appeared to stand out in puffy relief, making the pattern even more dramatic.

Another form of white work was a quilt, as above, but it had the designs stuffed individually with cotton or cord from the back. A small area of the textile was forced open to receive the stuffing and then the opening was worked back into place with the head of the needle. After laundering, the fabric closed back completely. This type of sculpturing is referred to as *trapunto* or *stuffed work*. Marseilles spreads, a French invention of the nineteenth century, reproduced this effect on a white machine-made cover which is highly collectible today.

BRODERIE PERSE

This was a seventeenth-century technique which reached its peak between 1820 and 1840. Only the affluent housewife could afford to make these covers.

Motifs of flowers, vines, peacocks, and pheasants were cut from chintz and appliquéd on a foundation, usually white, and then highlighted with embroidery. The ground was then quilted in a variety of stitches to the backing, without stuffing. The chintz was ordered from England, usually no more than one or two yards at a time, and carefully planned to conserve every last scrap. The center was usually a Tree of Life motif, influenced by printed fabrics made in India. The pattern was one dimensional since the tree had to face in an upright position. These covers were made for show and rarely used. The majority were made in the East and South.

ALBUM QUILTS

These quilts were usually created by a number of women who would each make a square; each square had an *appliquéd* design of their choice. These would often be made as a friendship effort and each square would be signed by one woman who "had a fine hand," some in ink and some in embroidery. Sometimes the entire quilt would be designed by a woman who was especially talented and the design for each square would be parcelled out to individual makers. There were some made by just one quilter who wanted a variety of patterns in her quilt rather than have each pattern exactly the same. These can usually be identified by the uniformity of design or work. These quilts are very interesting for the purpose of their design. Some were made as farewell gifts; some, known as Freedom Quilts, were made for young men when they became twenty-one or when they finished their apprenticeships; others were intended for young women who were planning their weddings.

It is said that the most beautiful quilts made in America are the "Baltimore" album quilts, made by a group of women in that area who were experts in needlework. They have several characteristic designs, including baskets of flowers, fruits, animals, and Baltimore monuments.

SAMPLER ALBUM

These quilts are very much the same as album quilts, except that the squares are *pieced* instead of being appliquéd. They were made by groups of women or by one woman, not necessarily in the Baltimore area. Some were signed, and some were not.

AMISH/MENNONITE

The Amish settled in Lancaster County, Pennsylvania, and some eventually moved into Indiana, Ohio, Illinois, Missouri, and Iowa. Because of their plain ways, their quilts have a simplicity of pattern which is relieved by the striking colors and the exquisitely designed and stitched quilting. The Amish religion forbade certain bright colors for clothing, such as pink, orange, and bright red, so they expressed themselves by the colors used in their quilts. And because of that strict lifestyle, very few quilts were made before 1860. Before that time, it is believed that the women wove stout wool blankets, or they stitched several layers of fabric together for extra warmth. Since the Amish have an oral history, most information is gained through conversations with the older women, so this is not documented. Most of the traditional Amish quilts were made between 1870 and the 1930s. Almost all quilts made after 1860 can be dated by the use of the sewing machine (foot-treadle, not electric!) for piecing. Also, almost all of the designs have straight edges and any of the basic three shapes: square, triangle, and rectangle. The quilting was always by hand and the early quilting frequently had twenty stitches to the inch, done entirely in black thread. Look for patterns of large diamonds inside squares, squares inside diamonds and triangles, plain squares, bars, bars inside squares, bars outlining solids, and many other such arrangements.

Originally, the Amish got almost all of their quilt fabrics from worn clothing and from the scrap basket. These were all colored with home-made dyes on homespun fabrics. In the late nineteenth century, they purchased fabrics at special stores that catered to the Amish needs. At this time there was a subtle change in the fabrics and dye colors used in the quilts.

Today there is a rainbow of colors to choose from, including subtle prints. Solid colors are always used for the top, although small prints and checks may be used on the backing in strips with other prints or solids. Quilts made for sale may have printed pieces in the tops, but not in quilts to be used in the Amish homes. Early stuffing was of wool, then cotton batting. Polyester is used today because it launders easier and dries more quickly, but the hand-stitching is not as fine because of the bulk of the polyester. The colors used in the construction of quilts are still stunning and individual to the Amish, but not as quaint, naive, and dramatic as in earlier quilts.

FRIENDSHIP

Friendship quilts are in the same category as the earlier Album quilts—pieced, signed, and dated. Most are made for friends, such as the rector of a church, a friend who is moving away, or a special citizen who is being honored. Many of these were done by a group of women who charged a small fee for each square, or the quilt was raffled to raise money. Whatever small amount realized from the sale was always used for a charitable cause. These quilts were also referred to as autograph, signature, tithing, and charity quilts.

COMMEMORATIVE/PATRIOTIC

From the late eighteenth into the late nineteenth century, there were quilts made to honor famous people or some special event in our country's history. Many were pieced-work quilts, and into the late nineteenth century some were crazy quilt designs with the person's image in the center or in some other way worked into the design. At the time of this country's centennial, patriotic quilts were popular. All of these quilts had flags and/or eagles as the major design element. Many of these quilts were made with campaign ribbons of political figures; some were made with kerchiefs which were printed with popular figures of the day.

HAWAIIAN

Until the early nineteenth century, sewing was unknown to these island people. In 1820, women of rank were given calico and were set to work learning to sew; their teacher was Mrs. Lucy Thurston, an American missionary. Sewing was allowed for only the most important women, according to rigid social standards. Because of their wealth, women always purchased fabric specifically for a planned design and never resorted to the scrap bag.

The majority will be of two types—patriotic, showing their flag, or commemorative, representing some special event. The work is always appliquéd, frequently using reverse appliqué. The early quilts are known for their striking colors and original designs. Many of the stylized floral quilts are evenly balanced by folding the fabric four ways and then cutting the design, similar to paper cutting, producing an original motif to appliqué onto the ground cloth. The quilting is usually done closely following the outline design of the center motif. The majority of early Hawaiian quilts are in museums and rarely appear on the market.

CRAZY QUILTS

When or why women in the United States started making crazy quilts seems to be debatable. Some may have been influenced by the Japanese displays at the Centennial Exhibition in Philadelphia; there many beautiful silks were shown for bed dressings, as well as elegant silk-screens. Many were also influenced by the Aesthetic Movement. Whatever the reason, by the middle of the 1880s there was tremendous interest in making these quilts using silks, satins, velvets, painted fabrics, ribbons, and clothing. A favorite with many women were men's silk ties, which they collected from family and friends. Many companies advertised packets of silks and the various embroidery threads used to decorate the squares.

These quilts were not constructed as the traditional patchwork quilts had been. The maker started with a square of plain fabric, an old piece of sheeting, calico or whatever was handy, and the free-form pieces of silk were basted down with the edges turned under and whipped into place. When the square was covered, the seams were then worked over with a variety of embroidery stitches using silk floss. Frequently, the pieces in the square had a design embroidered with the floss or chenille. Some were decorated with roses made from ribbons or small appliquéd designs which had been stuffed, and some were decorated with embroidered names of friends. The squares were seamed together and had a backing attached without quilting. Many women made fancy backs which were quilted separately in intricate designs before attaching. The bindings were often silk or velvet. Because of the rich colors and fabrics chosen for these quilts, they are handsome jewel-like creations. This craze continued well into the early twentieth century.

KITS AND PATTERNS

After the fad of the crazy quilt had died down in the early part of the twentieth century, interest in quilt making waned. Women had lost their desire for making the traditional patterns since the excitement of the crazy quilt, and machine-made blankets and bedcoverings were now available in the market. With World War I and the interest in Women's Suffrage, many women were not content to sit home and sew. However, by 1920, kits and printed patterns for both pieced and appliquéd quilts were made popular by many of the magazines published for the homemaker. Kits contained the pattern and frequently all the materials necessary to make and complete a quilt. Many kits had the fabrics ready-cut, requiring only piecing together by following printed instructions. Printed patterns were made available for use with each choice of fabric selected by the quilter.

Many quilts show great originality by the manner in which the quilter used these patterns and fabrics. Many fresh and attractive appliquéd quilt patterns became popular at that time, especially the florals with foliage and swags. The iris was especially popular. Kits were also available with the entire top done in embroidery. The pattern was printed on muslin and came with thread to complete the design. Kit and printed pattern quilts remained popular through the Depression and up to about 1940. With the war effort at that time, quilt making again lost favor, only to re-emerge in popularity during the 1960s and 1970s. It has now developed into an exciting and thriving business.

COLLECTING TIPS

To collect quilts or any other textile, it is important to be able to evaluate the age, condition, quality of fabric, workmanship, and aesthetic appeal, as well as be able to document the provenance. That sounds like a tall order to consider when planning the purchase of just one quilt. However, with prices escalating and the investment growing ever more precious, it is more than important to do your homework before attempting a final valuation.

Any museum in your area with a textile display will have facilities for research, and your local library has many references available. Visit antiques shops, shows, estate sales, flea markets, and any other sales in your area. Ask questions. Any legitimate antiques dealer will happily answer your questions and point you in the proper direction if he does not specialize in textiles; it's only good business and good will which is, after all, the heart of a successful business.

There is a bibliography at the end of this section with just a sampling of references. There are hundreds of books available at this time covering every conceivable subject relating to quilts and quilters.

Research, research, research! And remember: *no quilt is older than the youngest element in the original construction.*

Some things to consider:

• Look at the shape of the quilt. Earlier quilts were square or almost square because beds were shorter than what we consider standard size today. By mid-nineteenth century, quilts became more rectangular as beds became longer.

• Many quilts cannot be dated solely by the fabrics used. Some quilters saved scraps for ten to twenty years and then used fabric from cast-off clothing in the same quilt. Because of this, dating cannot be made by the worn appearance of the squares alone.

• Learn how to identify and test fibers to document fabrics; this will assist with dating (*see* Fibers in the "Glossary"). Be sure to shop with a strong magnifying glass.

• Early quilts were hand-quilted with as many as twenty stitches to an inch and were almost as even as machine-made quilts. American quilters used a running stitch, while English quilters favored a back stitch.

• Many older quilts were made with printed paper templates still stitched to the back of the pieces in the squares. These pieces of paper often have dates showing, or may be dated by subject matter or historical events mentioned. These quilts were obviously never expected to be laundered.

• By 1790, calico was woven in this country. It was usually of two colors with all-over small print, and it was used extensively for quilt making as well as clothing.

• Cotton batting has been used since the invention of the cotton gin in 1793. Quilts cannot be dated solely on the appearance of the cotton seed in the batting. Inexpensive unbleached batting with seeds was available into the early 1900s; and many women in the South made their own batting using gleanings from the fields. Wool batting was used in earlier quilts. Some may show stains from the natural lanolin in the wool. Always check the batting; sometimes an older quilt was used as batting and this may be more valuable than the outer quilt covering it.

• Before 1830, homemade inks were used to sign some quilts. Because these were made with rusted iron to "make them last," however, they will now be faded or will have corroded the fabric. By 1830, indelible inks were available.

• Prior to 1820, only natural dyes were used which were made from shellfish, insects, minerals, and plant matter. These colors gradually faded out into soft shades. By 1820, mineral dyes were being made; these were harsher than those made by natural matter.

• By 1856, synthetic coal-tar dyes produced a whole new range of brighter, more permanent colors.

• The sewing machine was introduced in 1860, and many women used it to piece the squares, although they hand-stitched the quilting. This fact does not greatly reduce the value of an old quilt that has been artfully designed and beautifully quilted. Even the Amish resorted to the sewing machine, but always hand-stitched the quilting. However, some serious collectors frown on machine-piecing.

• The early nineteenth century saw simple blue or red checks. Brown and color combinations were more rare.

• Housewives were still weaving a combination of machine-spun cotton thread and homespun linen as late as the third quarter of the nineteenth century, and you may still find quilts with this fabric.

• Pastels, such as pale pink, lavender, mint green, and turquoise became popular in the 1920s and into the 1940s.

• Check quilts for any alterations to bindings, replaced fabrics in squares or rebacking. The more original, the more valuable the quilt.

• Some repairs are acceptable if they do not destroy the integrity of the quilt. An old and fragile quilt with impeccable provenance may have moline used over thin pieces for protection, or minor tacking using thread of the period. (Moline is a thin transparent netting tacked over fragile pieces to prevent further splitting or loss, allowing the original colors to be visible.)

• An older cut-off quilt, still retaining all original fabric, is more desirable than a newer quilt which has alterations, such as new bindings.

• An Amish quilt made between 1920 and 1930 is considered to be more valuable than an earlier non-Amish quilt.

• On an important quilt, some discoloration and stain is acceptable. An expert conservationist may be able to remove it without damage to the quilt.

• Some minor wear and losses are acceptable on a fine example.

• Crib quilts are miniatures of larger quilts and should have a design that is in proportion to the smaller size. Check the binding to be sure it is original to the quilt and not added after a cut-down from a larger size. Examine the quilting from the back. If it is a cut-down version, the quilting will not balance with the overall design. Most crib quilts were made to be used and not many have survived the stress and launderings. Also, not as many were made originally as were larger quilts.

• Doll quilts are also miniatures. A popular design is the postage stamp, made with tiny one-inch square pieces. Most doll quilts will show the results of years of love. Before investing, be sure to check as you would with a crib quilt to be sure that it is not a cut-down or a remake. These charming small works of art make attractive wall hangings and are very desirable to the quilt collector and, even more so, to the doll collector.

QUALITY AND CONDITION KEYS

CONDITION KEYS

Measures only the physical condition of the article and not the quality of design, material or workmanship.

Fine Condition (FC): Near original condition or expertly restored to near original condition.

Good Condition (GC): No losses; no obvious major restorations; no cleaning needed. Ready to use or display.

Average Condition (AC): Small areas may need restitching; minor losses to fabric or binding; cleaning may be necessary. This is the condition in which most quilts are found.

Poor Condition (PC): Missing binding; losses to squares; fading, thinning, poor restorations, if any. Not collectible, but small areas may be used to make pillows, stuffed animals, pin cushions, etc.

QUALITY KEYS

Measures the stylishness and collectibility of the piece within its category.

Good Quality (GQ): Attractive, but fabrics and workmanship may not be of acceptable quality. Worthy of collecting for use, but not for investment.

Very Good Quality (VGQ): Fine fabrics, excellent stitchery in piecing and quilting; colors and fabrics arranged in an artistically pleasing manner.

Superior Quality (SQ): Workmanship of highest quality; all elements are superb and of the period; has stunning visual impact.

MARKET TRENDS

Renewed interest in the American quilt swept the country in the 1970s and 1980s and quilting became a major industry. Interest has remained on a high level ever since, although the market has fluctuated in the past several years. Many lovely quilts are going for $1,000 and less to the collector who wants a quilt to be used and enjoyed and not as a major investment. The first-time collector will thus find many affordable quilts— a large number are available out there! Many buyers today seem to resist going over that figure for average quality quilts.

The market trend for quilts between $1,000 and $6,000 seems to be a little slow unless they are quite exciting and of good quality and condition. As always, the finer offerings at the high end of the market always seem to sell, whatever the market trend. When an exceptional example comes on the market there are always serious collectors, decorators or investors who are interested.

Quilts from the nineteenth century are becoming more expensive, and Amish quilts, also of that period, are almost out of sight. The average collector is showing more and more interest in the examples made during the 1920s and 1930s, and there are some very attractive buys in that market today.

Major auction houses provide beautifully illustrated catalogs of their sales. They are very good indicators of market trends. These are available from the auction companies and also at your local library. A list of houses is found in the "Appendixes" of this book.

CARING FOR
YOUR QUILTS

It is very important that you protect your quilts, whether they are an inheritance or an investment. Each quilt is an individual work of art and can never be replaced. Each one deserves to be treated with great respect, protected and preserved for future generations. We are only interim caretakers.

There are varying opinions, even among experts, concerning the care and cleaning of quilts. Some believe they should be repaired and restored; some feel they should be left in original condition, that any restoration destroys the integrity of the quilt. The old, fragile, and priceless quilt should be evaluated by an expert conservationist/restorationist before *any* action is undertaken. There are many such services available. Several are listed at the end of this section, or you may check with your nearest museum conservator who can point you in the right direction.

STORING YOUR QUILTS

• To store quilts, fold with the top inside to prevent any fading. Always fold with plenty of acid-free tissue to help prevent any sharp creases. These may be placed in old well-laundered and rinsed pillow cases or old sheets. Acid-free textile storage boxes are highly recommended for this purpose to prevent weight of other quilts which may be stacked on top during storage. These boxes may be stacked on a closet shelf or slid under a bed if storage space is limited. Place a clear plastic envelope on the outside listing contents for easy retrieval.

• Refold quilts several times a year to prevent permanent creases which weaken the fabric.

• Never place a quilt or other textile on a wooden shelf without being protected by acid-free wrappings. Wood contains acids which will discolor and weaken the fibers.

• Do not store in plastic bags. Plastic will hold moisture and cause mildew to form. Attics have too wide a temperature range for fibers and possibly moisture. Basements are usually too moist and may cause mildew.

• Never allow mothballs to come in contact with wool quilts during storage.

• Always wear white cotton gloves when handling old quilts, especially fragile silks. Skin contains oils which may stain the fabric.

• Wood curtain rods or cardboard tubing, covered with quilted fabric which has been laundered and rinsed well, make good rolled storage for smaller quilts. Wrap with acid-free tissue or cover with a muslin sleeve. (Great for table linens also.)

• The three worst enemies of quilts are sunlight, moisture, and humidity.

CLEANING YOUR QUILTS

• I highly recommend an expert conservationist/restorationist to make any decision as to the proper way to handle an old, fragile or priceless quilt. Most quilts have many differing fabrics, dyes, and batting, and only an expert can determine how they will react to certain cleaning methods. An expert can document the age, fabrics, and condition of the quilt and determine what action, if any, should be undertaken.

• To dust a quilt, lay it flat on sheeting, cover with cheesecloth or gauze, and weight down beyond the edges of the quilt. Use a low-power vacuum cleaner setting, holding it at least three inches from the surface. Turn the quilt over and repeat on other side. Never use a vacuum without protection; it may loosen fragile fabric.

• Twentieth-century quilts made from synthetics and polyester batting may be laundered at home. First check all seams for any loose threads and repair if necessary. Use gentle cycle and a mild soap; rinse well to remove all residue of soap or detergent. Always dry flat, if possible, and on a piece of sheeting. This may be done outside in a shady spot. Line dry only if the quilt is sturdy and the wind is not too strong—and always out of the sun. A wet quilt is very heavy and the weight may cause splitting or tearing. Polyester batting dries more quickly than cotton.

• Cotton and linen quilts may be washed, but check colors for fastness. This is done by wetting a small spot and patting with a white cloth or blotter paper. Try each of the various colors, and do not forget the backing. If any stain shows on the cloth or paper, *don't wash*—have dry cleaned.

• A small object may be laundered in the bathtub. Use tepid water and mild soap. Do not scrub. Allow to soak and then swish in the water. To rinse, allow water to drain and add rinse water without removing the quilt. Rinse several times to remove all residue of soap. Do not twist or wring—press down on the wet mass to extract as much water as possible. Handle carefully while wet, and dry flat on sheeting.

• Wool and silk should never be washed. Check with an expert if you feel cleaning is absolutely necessary. Wool and silk may be dry cleaned if not fragile or old. Be sure to locate a cleaner who is trained in handling antique textiles.

DISPLAYING YOUR QUILTS

Quilts are considered an art form, and to be enjoyed they should be displayed and not kept tucked away. It is important to display them aesthetically for visual impact, and properly to protect them. Following are a few suggestions for preserving your quilts while living with them:

• Quilts which are not old or fragile may be spread on a bed or used on a lounge to cuddle in.

• Quilts make striking wall hangings, even large quilts when mounted properly. For quilts which are not too fragile, a simple sleeve may be hand stitched to the backing at one end. Run a flat curtain rod through the sleeve and hang. It is recommended that a sleeve be stitched at each end so that the quilt may be rotated several times a year to relieve the stress of hanging.

• Large quilts may have a backing of fabric hand-stitched on all four sides, and a few stitches running through the face of the quilt, at inconspicuous areas, to stabilize the entire quilt before adding the sleeves.

• A strip of lath run through the bottom sleeve will help keep the quilt even while hanging.

• Velcro is very convenient to use. Stitch one strip onto the sleeve and tack or glue one onto a strip of wood mounted on the wall, then just press into place.

• You may wish to mount the quilt on a frame. Hand-stitch a fabric lining on all four sides, leaving a margin. The margin will then be rolled over a frame and fastened without being visible. This stabilizes the quilt on all four sides.

• Drape your quilt over the back of a chair or sofa. Use as a table cover if it is protected by a waterproof liner over the quilt and then topped with a pretty linen cloth. You may use a quilt to cover the table for display, but never serve food or liquids without protection. That coffee stain may never come out!

• Never display your quilt in direct or reflected sunlight. Fluorescent lighting should not be used except with an ultraviolet filter.

• Be sure to keep quilts away from a heat source such as a radiator or heat vent, and never display near an air-conditioning vent to prevent moisture and mildew.

QUILTS LISTING

PATCHWORK QUILTS (APPLIQUÉD AND PIECED)

Apple Trees 79″ × 92″ Twentieth century United States
Appliquéd apple trees, birds, and meandering border in brown, red, green, and yellow. Embroidered stems. Somewhat faded. GQ/AC *$440 (A)*.... $300–$600

Blocks 76″ × 86″ Ca. 1920 North Carolina
Quilt top. Hand- and machine-pieced. 3″ blocks on diagonal, assorted jewel tones of rich blues, reds, and gold cotton fabrics. Unlined and unquilted. VGQ/FC *$125 (ES)* .... $50–$200

Blocks 75″ × 78″ Ca. 1900 North Carolina
Pieced. Blocks on diagonal; checked fabric, small prints, and old work shirt blue chambray; sashes of faded blue chambray and corner blocks of dark blue. Border of faded blue chambray, backed with Alamance County, NC, plaid cotton. Hand-quilted in all-over diamond pattern. *(See photo 88)* GQ/AC *$350 (D)* ....
.... $200–$500

Bow Tie 68″ × 80″ Ca. 1920 United States
Pieced. Calico and print on white squares with yellow calico ground and pink double-edge borders. Three ink-signed tapes stitched to quilt. Machine-sewn binding. Some overall fading and minor stains. GQ/AC *$220 (A)*.. $200–$400

Bow Tie 80″ × 88″ Ca. 1910 United States
Pieced. Red, teal green, and white. Scalloped border is teal green with red binding. Some faded areas in border. GQ/AC *$247.50 (A)* .... $200–$400

Carolina Lily 92″ × 101″ Ca. 1890–1910 United States
Appliquéd and pieced. The lily in red calico, solid green with green and blue sawtooth borders, and red calico binding. Beautifully quilted with vintage border. Signed in ink: "Sarah Elizabeth Beams." Very minor wear. *(See photo 89)* VGQ/FC *$1,237.50 (A)* .... $1,000–$2,000

PHOTO 88

PHOTO 89

PHOTO 90

Carolina Lily 79½″ × 78″ Ca. 1840–1850 Pennsylvania
Appliquéd, pieced, and stuffed. Worked in sixteen blocks of appliquéd flowers alternating with nine blocks of trapunto-stuffed squares repeating the lily design. Yellow lilies, green calico stems and leaves. Surrounded by green calico appliquéd swags. SQ/FC *$4,235 (A)*.. $2,500–$5,000

Diamond in Square 79″ × 79″ Ca. 1860 United States
Pieced. All calico with other prints in reds and other colors on a blue and white ground. Sawtooth border. Blue and white homespun backing. VGQ/GC *$880 (A)*.. $500–$1,200

Dresden Plate 14″ × 14″ Ca. 1920–1930 United States
Twenty-five quilt squares, unassembled. Hand-pieced in 1920's calico in assorted colors of yellows, reds, and greens. VGQ/FC *$5 Each, Never Used (ES)*.......
....$3–$25 Each

Eight-Point Star 80″ × 80″ Ca. 1900 Northampton County, Pennsylvania
Variation of nine-patch square. Pieced and quilted by hand. Polka dots, and prints in pinks, reds, and greens. Sashed in pink polka dots and green, triple border of pink, polka dots, and green. Backed with pink-striped cotton. (*See photo 90*)
SQ/FC *$1,250 (D)* ....$750–$1,500

> This is a good example showing a pattern achieved by rearranging fabrics and colors in a nine-patch square.

Floral 92″ × 90″ Ca. 1860 United States
Stylized floral medallions, appliquéd and pieced, in reds and greens. Some wear and fading; reds are more worn and have holes. GQ/PC *$160 (A)*.. $150–$500

Floral 92″ × 94″ Ca. 1850 United States
Stylized floral design in teal green and red calico. Beautifully quilted with floral designs between appliquéd medallions. Homespun backing. Minor age stains. VGQ/GC *$2,090 (A)* ....$1,500–$4,000

> The CONDITION KEY measures only the physical condition of the article and not the quality of design, material or workmanship.
> **Fine Condition (FC):** Near original condition or expertly restored to near original condition.
> **Good Condition (GC):** No losses; no obvious major restorations; no cleaning needed. Ready to use or display.
> **Average Condition (AC):** Small areas may need restitching; minor losses to fabric or binding; cleaning may be necessary. This is the condition in which most quilts are found.
> **Poor Condition (PC):** Missing binding; losses to squares; fading, thinning, poor restorations, if any. Not collectible, but small areas may be used to make pillows, stuffed animals, pin cushions, etc.
>
> The QUALITY KEY measures the stylishness and collectibility of the piece within its category.
> **Good Quality (GQ):** Attractive, but fabrics and workmanship may not be of acceptable quality. Worthy of collecting for use, but not for investment.
> **Very Good Quality (VGQ):** Fine fabrics, excellent stitchery in piecing and quilting; colors and fabrics arranged in an artistically pleasing manner.
> **Superior Quality (SQ):** Workmanship of highest quality; all elements are superb and of the period; has stunning visual impact.

PHOTO 91

PHOTO CREDIT: GARTH'S AUCTIONS, INC.

Floral 82″ × 82″   Ca. 1830–1850   United States
Appliquéd stylized flower pots of vining flowers in pink and green calico, with
solid red and yellow. (*See photo 91*) GQ/AC *$715 (A)* .... $500–$1,000
Floral 82″ × 96″   Ca. 1870–1880   United States
Appliquéd, twenty-six green flower pots, each with a different colored flower
and two blue calico birds. Green Greek key border. Minor stains. GQ/AC *$770*
(A) .... $500–$1,000
Floral 92″ × 94″   Ca. 1870   United States
Appliquéd stylized floral medallions with berries and meandering feather-stitched
trapunto design. Green calico and solid red and yellow floss embroidery stems
and berries. Some wear, small stains, binding has minor repair, and reds have a
few holes. (*See photo 92*) GQ/AC *$825 (A)* .... $500–$1,000

PHOTO 92

PHOTO CREDIT: GARTH'S AUCTIONS, INC.

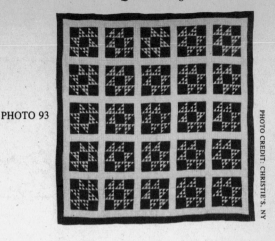

PHOTO 93

PHOTO CREDIT: CHRISTIE'S, NY

Flower Basket 80″ × 86″ 1875–1890 United States
Appliquéd and stuffed. Cotton with yellow basket of pink flowers, green leaves on white background. Arranged with eight squares having quilting of similar baskets. Green binding. Slight wear. VGQ/GC *$2,500 (D)*..... $1,500–$3,500
Flying Geese 82″ × 82″ Ca. 1870 Lincolnton County, Massachusetts
Pieced. Worked with twenty-five blocks in printed fabric on green ground, framed in white sashing with green border. Border quilted in chevrons. Small areas of staining and slight fading. *(See photo 93)* VGQ/AC *$1,089 (A)*.. $800–$1,500
Geese in Flight 84″ × 84″ Ca. 1890 United States
Pieced. Four bars, blue and white. Very good quilting. Overall wear. GQ/AC *$550 (D)* .... $350–$750
Log Cabin 77″ × 77″ Ca. 1880 Lehigh County, Pennsylvania
Pieced. "Barn raising" design, a variety of light and dark calicos and other prints in shades of tans, brown, and reds. Backed with 7″-wide strips of dark red and blue with white polka dots. Very fine stitching in piecing and quilting. *(See photo 94)* VGQ/FC *$1,500 (D)* .... $1,000–$2,000
Lone Star 78″ × 78″ Ca. 1875 United States
Pieced in red, goldenrod, and khaki on white ground. Red backing and binding. Well quilted. Overall wear, minor staining. GQ/AC *$450 (D)* ...... $300–$600
Mariner's Compass 76″ × 76″ Ca. 1880 United States
A variant of "Mariner's compass." Hand-appliquéd and pieced of red cotton fabric and white muslin. The squares create a white quatrefoil and have quilting to follow the design. Bordered and edged in sawtooth design. Border finely quilted in herringbone. This is a striking design, well executed. *(See photo 95)* SQ/FC *$4,500 (D)*.. $2,500–$5,000
Poinsettia 72″ × 90″ Ca. 1900–1910 United States
Appliquéd and pieced. Red, green, and gold on white ground. Twelve blocks of stylized poinsettias interspersed with white blocks similarly quilted. Floral swag border quilted in diaper stitch. VGQ/AC *$1,331 (A)* .... $1,200–$2,200
Sawtooth 68″ × 75″ Ca. 1860–1870 United States
This pattern is also known as "Kansas troubles." Pieced in alternating triangles with sawtooth edges on two sides. Blue calico and white homespun. GQ/AC *$715 (A)*.. $500–$800

PHOTO 95

PHOTO 94

Schoolhouse 69″ × 85″ Ca. 1900–1910 United States
Pieced. Each house has two shades of brown; blue sky, red chimney, and win-
dows are in calico and ecru. Brown print background with ruffled edge. Summer
weight, quilted without batting, ¼″-dia. burn hole. GQ/AC *$440 (A)* ....
.... $350–$750
Sixteen Patch 68″ × 80″ Ca. 1890 Alamance County, North Carolina
"Hired hand" quilt, all wool squares from clothing, dark colors, hand-pieced,
crudely quilted. Backed with Alamance County cotton plaid in navy and brown.
All corners were rounded off when repaired. PQ/AC *$150 (D)* .... $50–$150
Star 88″ × 88″ Ca. 1900 United States
Pieced, all in calico. Yellow and pink on green ground. Reversible with yellow
and pink bars on back. VGQ/AC *$935 (A)* .... $500–$1,500
Starburst 7′6″ × 9′ Ca. 1850 Southern United States
Because of the large size, this is known as a 'family bed" quilt, fitting a large
bed where any number of family members slept together. Deep rose, cream, and
goldenrod on white muslin. Goldenrod sashes and border. White muslin back.
Hand-pieced and quilted fourteen stitches to the inch. (*See photo 96*) VGQ/
FC *$1,800 (D)* .... $1,500–$2,500

PHOTO 96

PHOTO 97

Star of Bethlehem 82″ × 82″ Ca. 1880 Lehigh County, Pennsylvania
Full-field eight-point star, surrounded by smaller stars and pinwheels. Burnt
orange, red, yellow, and blue cotton and calico. Backed in white cotton with red
pin dots. Cotton batting with seeds. Hand-pieced, rope design quilting in border.
(See photo 97) VGQ/AC *$1,650 (D)* .... $1,200–$2,000

Sunshine and Shadow 76″ × 76″ Ca. 1880 Berks County, Pennsylvania
Machine-pieced, hand-quilted. All solid colors of cotton in a variety of shades.
Backed with 7″ strips of blue and brown calico prints. Seeds in thin cotton
batting. *(See photo 98)* GQ/FC $900 (D).............................$750–$1,200

PHOTO 98

PHOTO 100

PHOTO 99

Triangles 84″ × 84″ Ca. 1890 Pennsylvania
Also known as "thousand pyramids." All blocks are triangles of assorted calico
and solid fabrics in light and dark shades. Browns predominate. Hand-pieced
and quilted. *(See photo 99)* VGQ/FC *$2,000 (D)*.................. $1,500–$2,500

> At first glance, this quilt would appear to be a log cabin pattern. Look closely
> and you will see triangles instead of narrow rectangular pieces as in a log
> cabin. A visually stunning quilt, it would lend itself well to hanging.

Tumbling Blocks 48″ × 60″ Ca. 1890 New Jersey
Hand-pieced. All velvet and silk in tones of burgundy, mauve, and rose. The
backing is of burgundy-color cotton, exquisitely quilted in all-over floral design
with princess feather border. Not quilted to front. Sleeved for hanging. Several
of the silk pieces are beginning to split. *(See photo 100)* FQ/GC *$450 (D)*.....
.... $350–$750

WHITE WORK, WHOLE CLOTH

Bride's Quilt 86″ × 86″ Ca. 1890 United States
White work, whole cloth, all-white muslin, finely quilted all over with highly
designed center of floral and vining motif; border with princess feather quilting.
Thin batting. SQ/FC *$2,500 (D)*.....................................$1,000–$5,000
Bride's Quilt 88″ × 90″ Ca. 1900 United States
Whole cloth, white-on-white beautifully quilted floral with urns and vintage bor-
der. GQ/AC *$725 (A)* .... $500–$1,200
Whole Cloth 72″ × 90″ Ca. 1940 United States
Mauve rayon, hand-quilted overall in geometric design. Scalloped edges. Thin
cotton batting. GQ/AC *$50 (ES)* ....$25–$150

PHOTO 101

ALBUM QUILTS

Album 85″ × 95″ Ca. 1850 Maryland
Appliquéd and pieced; center a square reserve with a lemon tree, the inner border with thirty-eight pictorial squares including tulips, roses, oak leaves, flower baskets, wreaths, birds, and flags; surrounded by a floral swag border. Slight staining. One-dimensional tree. (*See photo 101*) SQ/FC *$6,050 (A)*..............
.... $5,000–$10,000

AMISH/MENNONITE

Barred 80″ × 94″ Ca. 1880 Berks County, Pennsylvania
Amish. Cotton in shades of dark green, light orange, and mahogany brown, bordered with dark green; backed with red calico print. All-over diamond quilting in eighteen stitches per inch. Thin cotton batting. (*See photo 102*) VGQ/AC *$1,200 (D)* ....$750–$1,500

PHOTO 102

Checkerboard 85″ × 87″ Ca. 1900 United States
Amish, pieced quilt. Black and maroon. Some wear, maroon is frayed in places
and black wool has some moth holes. (Black squares are of a variety of fabrics
including sateen, wool, and crepe.) GQ/PC *$165 (A)*................. $100–$500

> You will frequently find a variety of fabrics in a single color, as with the
> blacks above, in an Amish or Mennonite quilt. Often a piece will be on bias
> within the same strip with a straight-cut piece.

Joseph's Coat-of-Many-Colors 84″ × 90″ Ca. 1880 Lancaster County,
Pennsylvania
Mennonite, pieced quilt. Bars in a spectrum of bright fabrics with rope-twist
stitching, the border similarly stitched, with purple binding. (*See photo 103*) SQ/
FC *$6,050 (A)*... $2,500–$7,500
Lightning Bolt 80″ × 80″ Ca. 1940 Middlefield, Ohio
Amish, pieced quilt. Wool and corduroy. Vivid colors with deep blues, greens,
reds, black, etc. Made by Fannie Detweiler. Stains, some bleeding of color, and
small holes. GQ/PC *$385 (A)*........................... $350–$1,000
Old Maid's Puzzle 80″ × 94″ Ca. 1950 United States
Amish, pieced quilt. Two shades of blue and light green. Hand-sewn with
machine-sewn binding. Some loose seams, small holes, and minor stains. GQ/
PC *$75 (A)*...$50–$250
Princess Star Feather 72″ × 90″ Ca. 1880 Lancaster County,
Pennsylvania
Mennonite, appliquéd and pieced. Worked in four blocks; in mustard and green
fabric on red ground with floral baskets along the center in similar fabrics; within
a sawtoothed frame with a green border with rope-twist stitching. Some fading
and minor staining. One-dimensional basket in center. (*See photo 104*) VGQ/
AC *$2,860 (A)*.....................................$2,000–$5,000
Sunshine and Shadow 81″ × 81″ Ca. 1930–1935 Kokomo, Indiana
Amish, pieced quilt. Pattern in all solid colors. Made by Denise Katie Hersch-
burger. Machine-sewn and hand-quilted. Small tear in one blue block. GQ/
AC *$412.50(A)*... $350–$1,000

PHOTO 103

PHOTO 104

PHOTO 105

FRIENDSHIP

Friendship 77″ × 78″ 1904 Lehigh County, Pennsylvania
Hand-pieced. Light blue and white blocks, 5½″ blue calico border, backed in
rich red and orange calico in 8″ strips. Almost all of the blocks are signed and
dated in ink. Corner block shows "Presented to Charles G. Beck, Pastor, St.
Peter's Lutheran Church, North Wales, Pa., 1904. Made by the Ladies of the
Church." Later inscription to grandson (of the same name), "Presented to
Charles G. Beck, 1914, by Great-Great Grandmother Herman." Finely hand-
quilted; thin cotton batting. (*See photo 105*) VGQ/GC *$900 (D)* .$750–$1,200
Friendship 65″ × 78″ Ca. 1890–1890 Kentucky
Pieced. Multicolor prints and white with penciled names. Good overall condition
except for olive brown fabrics which are faded and frayed. GQ/AC *$605 (A)*..
....$750–$1,200

COMMEMORATIVE

Trip Around the World 77″ × 80″ 1876 Philadelphia
Pieced quilt, with several patches having busts of Washington, "Union" 1776–
1876, etc. Back has colorful red paisley print. Made at the Centennial. GQ/
AC *$440 (A)* .... $300–$750

The CONDITION KEY measures only the physical condition of the article and not the quality of design, material or workmanship.

Fine Condition (FC): Near original condition or expertly restored to near original condition.

Good Condition (GC): No losses; no obvious major restorations; no cleaning needed. Ready to use or display.

Average Condition (AC): Small areas may need restitching; minor losses to fabric or binding; cleaning may be necessary. This is the condition in which most quilts are found.

Poor Condition (PC): Missing binding; losses to squares; fading, thinning, poor restorations, if any. Not collectible, but small areas may be used to make pillows, stuffed animals, pin cushions, etc.

The QUALITY KEY measures the stylishness and collectibility of the piece within its category.

Good Quality (GQ): Attractive, but fabrics and workmanship may not be of acceptable quality. Worthy of collecting for use, but not for investment.

Very Good Quality (VGQ): Fine fabrics, excellent stitchery in piecing and quilting; colors and fabrics arranged in an artistically pleasing manner.

Superior Quality (SQ): Workmanship of highest quality; all elements are superb and of the period; has stunning visual impact.

HAWAIIAN

Floral   78″ × 80″   Ca. 1850   Hawaii
Appliquéd. Worked with four enlarged floral and vine urns in blue fabric with white dots on a white ground; echo stitching and slate blue binding. (*See photo 106*) VGQ/FC   *$5,500 (A)* .... $3,000–$7,500

PHOTO 106

PHOTO CREDIT: CHRISTIE'S, NY

PHOTO CREDIT: CHRISTIE'S, NY

PHOTO 107

Patriotic 74″ × 74″ Ca. 1860–1880 Hawaii
Appliquéd. Center a square reserve depicting the crest of the Hawaiian monarchy and inscribed "KUU HAE" ("My beloved flag") above and "ALOHA" below, surrounded by four stylized Hawaiian flags. Completed with four blue triangles and a white binding (worn). (*See photo 107*) VGQ/GC *$8,800 (A)* ....
.... $5,000–$10,000

CRAZY QUILTS

Crazy Quilt 84″ × 86″ Ca. 1900 United States
Charming primitive. Pieced of old, dark wool fabrics, probably from men's suits. Wool embroidery between each square; family members' handprints embroidered on pieces. Signed "Willie Mae." Slight wear. GQ/AC *$150 (ES)* ....
.... $100–$350
Crazy Quilt 74″ × 76″ Ca. 1900 United States
Pieced. All wool in assorted designs, jewel-like tones of blues, mauve, rose, beige, goldenrod, etc. Heavy wool embroidery. Back of mauve sateen, finely quilted in geometric pattern, separately. Size above plus 4″ mauve ruffle on four sides. A very heavy quilt. (*See photo 108*) GQ/AC *$450 (D)* .... $350–$500
Crazy Quilt 76″ × 80″ Ca. 1900–1910 Orange County, North Carolina
Pieced. All wool, dark colors, probably from clothing. Each piece with wool embroidery of flowers. Much damage to wool. GQ/PC *$25 (ES)* ..... $25–$150
Crazy Quilt 84″ × 92″ Ca. 1890 United States
Pieced. Combination of silks, wools, and velvets in various rich colors. Silk floss embroidery of birds, butterflies, animals, fans, etc. Bound in dark red silk. Some wear to silk pieces. VGQ/AC *$750 (D)* .... $500–$1,200

PHOTO 108

PHOTO 109

PHOTO 110

PHOTO 111

Crazy Quilt Hanging 18″ × 36″ Ca. 1900 United States
Pieced. Two squares seamed to make wall hanging. All assorted silks with silk embroidery, chenille daisy, and bluettes, 2″-wide black silk border. Sleeved at top for hanging. One silk piece splitting. (*See photo 109*) VGQ/AC *$125 (D)*
.... $50–$150

Crazy Quilt Squares 14″ × 14″ each Ca. 1900–1910 Reading, Pennsylvania
Pieced. All silk, various rich colors from men's ties; satin, painted silk, etc. Embroidered with silk floss, some with chenille roses and daisies. (*See photos 110 and 111*) VGQ/FC *$30 Each (ES)* .... $25–$45 Each

KITS/PATTERNS

Checkerboard 78″ × 92″ Ca. 1930–1935 United States
Pieced; from a pattern. Blue and white squares alternating. The white squares are embroidered with bright flowers and butterflies. Blue binding. Hand-quilted; cotton batting. GQ/AC *$375 (D)* .... $250–$500

Iris 80″ × 92″ Ca. 1930 United States
Appliquéd. From a kit. Iris in several shades of lavender and deep purple, embroidered yellow centers, green leaves in several shades; on white muslin ground, bound in green. Hand-quilted in open spaces in floral pattern. GQ/AC *$450* *(D)*.. $250–$500

Sunbonnet Babies 68″ × 86″ Ca. 1935 United States
From a printed pattern. Squares alternate with appliquéd babies in colorful calico and white squares with embroidered flowers. Predominantly pinks and greens. White muslin squares. Cotton batting. Some fading of colors. GQ/AC *$75* *(ES)* .... $50–$250

Sunflowers 78″ × 94″ Ca. 1945–1950 United States
Appliquéd. Sunflowers and border stripe in green, yellow, and brown on a white ground. Unused condition with pencil quilting pattern intact. Small tear near one corner. GQ/AC *$385.50 (A)* .... $250–$500

CRIB QUILTS

Amish 30″ × 45″ Contemporary Ohio
Pieced. Blue, black, and gray. Machine-pieced and hand-quilted. GQ/ AC *$247.50 (A)*.. $150–$350

Amish—Lone Star 43″ × 43″ 1965 Holmes County, Ohio
Lone star in bright colors on a black ground. Made by Sarah Miller. GQ/ AC *$165 (A)*... $150–$350

Blocks 35″ × 41″ 1930–1940 United States
Pieced. Printed chintz; floral pattern with patchwork design; in shades of brown and green on white, alternating dark and light. One end faded. GQ/AC *$82.50* *(A)*... $50–$125

Double Star 34″ × 40″ Ca. 1860 United States
Hand-pieced. Red and brown print calico on white muslin ground, white muslin back. Finely hand-quilted. Cut down to crib size and fringe added in 1900. Well-balanced stars and quilting in the alteration. Quilted eighteen stitches per inch. *(See photo 112)* VGQ/AC *$175 (D)* .... $100–$300

PHOTO 112

Gingerbread Children 36″ × 48″ Ca. 1930 United States
Appliquéd, from a kit. Center with gingerbread-colored fabric, appliquéd house surrounded by gingerbread boys and girls in same fabric; details on clothing in white rick-rack braid. White muslin ground. White backing with gingerbread binding. Thin cotton batting. Small block quilting in ground. A charming quilt— would look great hung in a child's room. VGQ/AC *$245 (D)* .... $150–$350
Monkey Wrench 31″ × 42½″ Ca. 1900–1910 LaGrange, Indiana
Pieced; reversible. Monkey wrench in blue, red, and white on one side, nine-patch on the other in various color prints on the same blue ground. Made by Edythe Cole. VGQ/AC *$495 (A)*... $350–$600
Sawtooth 54″ × 54″ Ca. 1935 Carbon County, Pennsylvania
Pieced. Blue calico and white muslin. Finely quilted in all-over ½″ diagonal pattern. Thin cotton batting. Labeled "Made by the Ladies of Trinity Lutheran Church, Bowmanstown, Pennsylvania." Blues are faded. GQ/AC *$225(D)* ....
.... $150–$300

DOLL QUILTS

Flying Geese 21½″ × 26″ Ca. 1930–1940 United States
Pieced. "Flying geese" pattern in orange and white. Machine-sewn. Overall wear, fading, and tear to one "goose." GQ/PC *$66 (A)*.............. $50–$100
Four-Patch 17″ × 25″ Ca. 1920–1930 United States
Pieced and knotted. Four-patch in blues and other prints. GQ/PC *$22 (A)*.....
.... $20–$50
Nine-Patch 13½″ × 13½″ Ca. 1890 United States
Hand-pieced in assorted calicos and checks. Sashes, backing, and binding of maroon print calico. Thin cotton batting; quilting is primitive. Much loved condition. *(See photo 113)* GQ/PC *$25 (ES)*................................... $20–$50
Postage Stamp 13½″ × 19½″ Ca. 1890 United States
Hand-pieced, 1″ squares of assorted calicos and other fabrics in a variety of colors. Backed and bound in burgundy and white print calico. Thin cotton batting; hand-quilted. Minor fading and wear. *(See photo 114)* GQ/AC *$65 (ES)* .... $45–$125
Tumbling Blocks 16¾″ × 19½″ Ca. 1920 United States
Hand-pieced. Colorful satins. Wear and stains with some damage. Red has bled in places. *(See photo 115)* GQ/PC *$49.50 (A)* .... $25–$75

PHOTO 113   PHOTO 114

PHOTO 115

PHOTO CREDIT:
GARTH'S AUCTIONS,
INC.

MUSEUMS

When planning a visit to a museum, be sure to call ahead and check the days and hours which they are open to the public. Some may be open only by appointment for individual inspection and some only by appointment for guided tours to view your special interest. Museums do not keep everything on view; most displays are on a rotating schedule. It is recommended that you check their schedule before making a special trip.

There are many fine museums around the country—too many to list here. Those listed are just a sampling and suggestion for your further research.

Abby Aldrich Rockefeller
Folk Art Center
Williamsburg, VA

Daughters of the American
Revolution (DAR) Museum
1776 D Street, N.W.
Washington, DC 20006

Greenfield Village and
Henry Ford Museum
Dearborn, MI

Henry Francis Du Pont Museum
Winterthur, DE

Honolulu Academy of Arts
Honolulu, HI

Kentucky Historical Society
Frankfort, KY

Museum of American Folk Art
New York, NY

National Museum of History
and Technology
Smithsonian Institution
Washington, DC

Shelburne Museum
Shelburne, VT

The Valentine Museum
1015 East Cary Street
Richmond, VA 23219

BIBLIOGRAPHY

Bacon, Lenice Ingram. *American Patchwork Quilts*. New York: Bonanza Books, division of Crown Publishing, Inc., 1980. Reprint of edition published by William Morrow, Inc., 1973. Mrs. Bacon has made historic background very enjoyable reading, even if you are not collecting quilts. Includes many color photographs.

Bishop, Robert. *New Discoveries in American Quilts*. New York: E. P. Dutton & Co., Inc., 1975.

Bishop, Robert, William Secord, and Judith Reiter Weisman. *The Knopf Collectors' Guide to American Antiques, Quilts, Coverlets, Rugs and Samplers*. New York: Alfred A. Knopf, 1982. Very informative and useful for the beginner. Handy pocket or purse size. Full color.

Bishop, Robert and Elizabeth Safanda. *A Gallery of Amish Quilts. Design Diversity From a Plain People*. New York: E. P. Dutton & Co., Inc., 1976. As much a history of the Amish as a study of their quilts, which brings a better understanding of their craft.

Brackman, Barbara. *Clues in the Calico*. McLean, Virginia: EPM Publications, 1990. An excellent new book containing information for dating quilts made between 1800 and 1950. Includes procedures for identification of fibers, fabrics, dyes, prints, techniques, etc. An essential reference for your library.

Duke, Dennis and Deborah Harding, editors. *America's Glorious Quilts*. New York: Park Lane, distributed by Crown Publishers, Inc., 1989. The title is correct! This is a gloriously illustrated book in large format. Encyclopedic, in ten chapters, each written by an expert.

Eanes, Ellen Fickling, et al. *North Carolina Quilts*. Edited by Ruth Haislip. North Carolina: Chapel Hill, The University of North Carolina Press and London, 1988. A massive undertaking by the North Carolina Arts Council. This is a study of the state's quilts and the women who made them. There are seven chapters, each written by a quilt expert.

Hinson, Delores A. *A Quilter's Companion*. New York: Arco Publishing Co., Inc., 1973. Explains the construction of a quilt and the necessary amount of materials needed. Also has a number of full-size patterns to trace for making appliquéd and pieced quilts. Includes a section on quilting motifs. Just reading this book will familiarize you with many of the popular quilt and quilting designs.

Safford, Carleton and Robert Bishop. *America's Quilts and Coverlets*. New York: E. P. Dutton & Co., Inc., 1972.

Woodward, Thomas K. and Blanche Greenstein. *Classic American Quilts*. New York: E. P. Dutton & Co., Inc., 1984. No text—just a visual treat. All color photographs.

———. *Crib Quilts and Other Small Wonders*. New York: E. P. Dutton & Co., Inc., 1981. A very informative book on this subject.

Coverlets

HISTORY

Woven coverlets were made in England before the first settlers came to this country. It is thought that coverlets came over with them as part of their household necessities; when those coverlets began to wear out, the housewife was forced to weave replacements. The loom was an integral part of the household, many coming from England with the settlers. Many were made here in this country—very simple affairs—from hewn logs, and they served the same intended purpose. All young girls were taught to spin and weave as a natural extension of their lives. Spinning and weaving went on whenever there was any spare time or when it became a necessity. Usually spinning was done during the summer months, and the busiest weaving time of year was from Christmas until Easter when the weather was not suitable for outside chores. During the warm months, the housewife was responsible for tending to the kitchen garden, chickens and farm animals, as well as to all of the other household duties.

The earliest looms were very basic and no fancy patterns could be woven on them. They could produce fine linen cloth, thin material for baby clothes and underwear, wool for clothing, wool and cotton coverlets for the beds, and heavy tow for bed and feed sacks and other farm use. It was possible to weave plaids, checks, and stripes by using colored yarns. Most produced narrow strips of fabrics no more than 40"–45" wide maximum, so it was necessary to seam strips together for beddings and tablecloths. Some fancy goods were imported from England, but for economic reasons, the early colonists depended on their own looms.

It is a wonder to us today that the housewife could put up her loom in a small cabin, no larger than a keeping room, and raise a family of up to twelve children in the same small space. Fortunately, the loom could easily be dismantled and the components stored in the loft until the next weaving time. The more prosperous families could afford a weaving room or a small building on the property. Many southern women taught slaves to weave the large quantities of fabrics and bedding necessary to run a large plantation or farm.

A coverlet was not made to be used as a counterpane, but as a utilitarian necessity—a warm bedcover or cover-lid (from the French *covrir lit*). The earliest made in this country were of a homespun linen warp with homespun and dyed wool weft. A few were made with wool in both the warp and weft, but, unfortunately, very few of these have survived.

Not many coverlets from the seventeenth and early eighteenth centuries have survived that can be definitely documented. The majority of what we see on the market today are made with cotton weft and wool warp from the late eighteenth century and the nineteenth century.

Machine-made coverlets date from the mid-nineteenth century. The mills were fully mechanized by that time, using water power. Many of these factories were located in the northeast and some in the mid-west. During the Civil War, factories were busy weaving blankets for the war effort and few had time to weave coverlets. When the war ended, hand-woven coverlets had lost favor to the manufactured blankets, although hand-weaving did continue in some rural areas for some time. Today, there are still many people who are interested in hand-weaving and are making coverlets, using the simple hand looms as used by their ancestors and copying many of the old patterns.

To avoid any misconceptions in terminology, quilts and coverlets are not the same and the terms are not interchangeable. A quilt is made by sewing fabrics together in three layers—a top, a middle batting for warmth, and a backing. These three layers are held together by stitching through all layers in a decorative or simple manner. Some of the more decorative quilts which are used especially for show have little or no middle batting and are in only two layers. A coverlet is made by weaving yarns together on a loom. Both are intended for use as warm bed coverings, and the early examples of both show the freshness and artistic inventiveness of the early settlers who sought warmth and beauty in a new and harsh land.

TYPES OF COVERLETS

There are four types of coverlets: overshot; double weave; summer and winter; and jacquard.

OVERSHOT

This is considered to be the first type of coverlet made in America. It was made on the simple, small hand loom, in strips of no more than 40″–45″ widths. Early coverlets had homespun linen as the warp thread and homespun and homedyed wool as the weft. The most popular color for the wool was various shades of indigo blue. Soon other colors became popular: reds from cochineal and madder; yellows from cosmos, onion skins, weld, and zinnias; greens from mixing weld with indigo; and browns from walnuts. The availability of cotton yarn replaced linen and very few coverlets with linen warp are found today.

The overshot pattern was achieved by having the wool weft skip over several of the warp threads at given spaces to create a pattern. The skip thread would lay on top of the warp and could be lifted up with a small implement or a fingernail, very much like a long stitch in bargello needlework. Because of these loose threads, overshot coverlets do not wear as well as other weaves. To strengthen the overshot weave, a cotton or linen thread was run across as a weft in between each of the wool weft threads, giving stability to the background. It was possible to weave many different designs and color combinations, although all were geometric or plaids.

With the narrow loom, the coverlet was woven in a long strip beginning at the bottom of the coverlet. When the design reached the top of the coverlet, a few inches would be woven of the plain linen and then the pattern would be reversed, continuing to weave downward to the bottom of the coverlet in one long piece. When it was removed from the loom, that middle area was cut and the two strips were stitched together down the center. The top was hemmed and the sides retained weft threads to be tied into fringe. Fringe for the bottom was woven separately and stitched on, except in the design of a plaid coverlet, where colored yarns would be coming from both warp and weft directions. Frequently, no attempt was made to match the design precisely down the center, although the pattern was reversed while weaving the second half of the strip to make matching possible.

No coverlets were signed in the loom. Sometimes there were cross-stitched initials or numbers worked on a corner after the coverlet had been completed and removed from the loom.

DOUBLE WEAVE

These coverlets were also made on a small, narrow hand loom and had to be seamed up the center. The weaving incorporated two warp yarns and two weft yarns that were woven back-to-back. Where there was a color change, the weft yarn would go through to the other layer of fabric, thus joining the two layers together at that color change. This produced a coverlet with a dark background with light pattern on one side and a light background on the other with dark pattern showing. The two layers could be separated with the fingers, and the two layers also made a very warm bedcover. All patterns were geometric and in colors available at the time. A few were initialed.

It is thought that double-weave coverlets date from about 1725 to 1825. However, surviving coverlets seem to date from the late eighteenth to the early nineteenth century. One weaver named James Alexander, a Scotsman who had passed rigid tests of the weavers' guild in his country before immigrating, announced himself as equipped to weave linen dam-

ask for tablecloths and double-weave carpets and coverlets. As with many
early weavers in this country who opened their own weaving business,
he was also a farmer. The earliest documented Alexander coverlet is
from 1805.

SUMMER/WINTER

This is a single-weave double-face coverlet. This type of weave has the
design in reverse from front to back. One side is light and presumably
used in summer; the other side is dark and used in winter. Since this is
lighter in weight than the double weave, it would be suitable for summer
use. The designs were more elaborate than the overshot, but still geometric, and they were also more closely woven, having the overshot pass
over no more than three warp threads at a time. To stabilize the ground,
a cotton weft thread was passed over each warp thread between each of
the wool weft rows. Many of the patterns closely resembled quilt designs, and like quilts, they were given names by the individual weavers.
You will find similar names for many different patterns in many different
parts of the country.

It was technically possible for the housewife to weave this type of
coverlet on her simple hand loom; however, because of the intricate
designs, they were almost all done by professional weavers. During the
early nineteenth century, many professional German weavers came to
this country, the majority settling in Pennsylvania. It is thought that they
developed this type of weave.

JACQUARD

This type of coverlet was made possible when a Frenchman, Joseph
Jacquard, invented an attachment for the loom that would make possible
patterns of curvilinear designs on large unseamed coverlets. The attachment could also be used on existing double-weave looms. It was a series
of punched cards, resembling player piano rolls, which activated the
harnesses of the loom and created the pattern as the coverlet was woven.
Since this required a large loom of great height and two men to operate
it, it was impossible to be used in a home by one person. Also, since it
did require specialized weavers to operate the mechanism, this saw the
end of much weaving in the home.

Jacquard coverlets could be woven in a variety of patterns and with
fanciful borders. These borders were often the specialized designs of one
particular weaver and usually contained his name, date, town, and customer's name in a corner block. This has greatly aided research into the
history, area of manufacture, and provenance of this type of coverlet.
There have been hundreds of jacquard weavers documented, many being

Germans who had immigrated to this country to better their opportunities. These weavers had pattern books to show their clients to assist in personalized designs and were trained to punch new cards to weave the new patterns. Many advertised this service and offered to dye the yarns to suit the customer. Today, these pattern books are highly collectible and are a valuable source for textile research. Some of the sheets in these pattern books closely resemble written sheet music.

The National Museum of History and Technology, Smithsonian Institution, Washington, DC, has a complete set-up showing a loom with a jacquard attachment, flax and wool in their original states, and dyeing material. The complete weaving process is shown all the way through to a completed coverlet still on the loom. It is worth a special trip if you are in the Washington, DC, area.

COLLECTING TIPS

As I have mentioned before, it is important to research what you are collecting. You must know the age, condition, and quality of your subject. You must know how to recognize patterns, workmanship, and dyes of the period, as well as the size of the looms producing the coverlets in that period. Learn to recognize the names and locations of some of the weavers. Then, when you are inspecting a coverlet at a shop, show or estate sale, you will have that all important *feel* of what you see before you. Is it aesthetically pleasing? Is the selection of colors exciting? Does it *speak* to you? Will you be happy living with it?

There is a bibliography at the end of this section for your use in further study and research. Many museums around the country have coverlets in their permanent collections and will be happy to accomodate you in your quest for further study.

Some things to consider are:

• Refer to Fibers in the "Glossary." This will assist you in determining age by recognizing fibers used. Be sure to shop with a strong magnifying glass. The oldest coverlets used hand-spun linen as the weft. The spinning jenny was invented in 1767 and made weaving with cotton easier for the housewife; however, many continued spinning their own home-raised flax into the early nineteenth century.

• Prior to 1820, only natural dyes were used which were made from shellfish, insects, minerals, and plant matter. These colors gradually faded into soft shades. By 1820, mineral dyes were being made which were harsher than those made with other natural matter.

• By 1856, synthetic coal-tar dyes introduced a new range of brighter, more permanent colors.

• The mid-nineteenth century saw the beginning of manufactured coverlets. These are more evenly woven and lack the soft *hand* as seen in hand-woven coverlets. The colors will not be as soft as with the older dyes. Older coverlets will show more wear, especially to the surface of the wool and to the fringe.

• In older coverlets, the area of greatest wear will show at the top end. These were made to be used as blankets, and after many years of being pulled up to cozy the chin much damage resulted to that area. Many have been rehemmed after losses, and many will show repairs in that area. Look for losses of fringe and the center being reseamed.

• Hold the coverlet up to the light and inspect it overall for moth damage to the wool and silverfish damage to the cotton or linen weft.

Moth damage is rampant and silverfish may be evident. Mildew and a musty smell are also frequent problems.

• New coverlets are being made on hand looms and are for sale in many specialty shops and through craft groups. These new coverlets are easily recognized by their fresh appearance, crisp feel, and brightness. Many are made with hand-dyed yarns, but will not have the look of age and wear.

• Coverlets were woven on narrow hand looms and sewn down the center until the advent of the jacquard loom, which then made possible wider one-piece covers after 1820.

• Jacquard coverlets were made in much greater numbers than coverlets made at home on hand looms; consequently, many more of these will be found on the market today. The older overshot will be less plentiful because of losses to the loose weave of the wool warp, and also because the housewife was not as prolific as professional weavers.

QUALITY AND CONDITION KEYS

CONDITION KEYS

Measures only the physical condition of the article and not the quality of design, materials used or workmanship.

Fine Condition (FC): As close to mint as possible; no stains or visible repairs; bright colors; no thin areas; no losses.

Good Condition (GC): Few repairs, using period threads and not obvious if repaired. All seams and hems are strong; original fringe or of the period if replaced. Colors good with slight fading of dyes; some overall wear.

Average Condition (AC): Some repairs, fading, and thinning. Minor breaks and losses. May need cleaning. This is the condition in which most are found.

Poor Condition (PC): Thinning and breaks in wool; some losses, especially at top; fading; needs cleaning. Not collectible for investment. If not valuable due to provenance, will be suitable for pillows, stuffed toys, and framed sections.

QUALITY KEYS

Measures the stylishness and collectibility of the piece within its category.

Good Quality (GQ): Nice piece worthy of collecting, but not for investing.

Very Good Quality (VGQ): Appealing design; good color selection; workmanship is excellent; all elements stylistically correct for period.

Superior Quality (SQ): High visual impact; expert workmanship of highest quality; all elements are superb and of the period.

MARKET TRENDS

Coverlets are a very popular item in the antiques and collectibles fields at present. The renewed interest in all textiles recently has caused the market to appreciate considerably. This trend has been helped along tremendously by various decorator and home magazines, as well as interior decorators. Many coverlets are more modestly priced than quilts of the same age and condition. It is still possible to collect some very attractive coverlets for under $500. Prices are stable at this time and probably will remain so for a while. But, just remember, as with all antique textiles, they are becoming more scarce and, with time, they will appreciate in value along with market demands. Always buy the very best for the amount you have to invest.

CARING FOR
YOUR COVERLETS

As with all antique textiles, coverlets are fragile and must be treated with respect. The wool will fade, is easily snagged and broken, and is a joyful feast to moths. Moths are probably the greatest threat to coverlets. The old cotton or linen yarns become brittle and break or rip with very little pressure, and, if dyed, the colors will fade. Here are a few things to consider in caring for your coverlets:

• Regarding cleaning, I would suggest most strongly to seek the advice of a professional. These fibers cannot bear the weight of being wet in laundering; since there is a combination of wool and either cotton or linen, laundering could thus be very tricky. The older dyes are not stable and could be ruined by wetting. If dry cleaning is a consideration, be sure to seek out a professional cleaner who is knowledgeable in the treatment of antique textiles.

• Regarding storage, always use acid-free tissue and acid-free storage boxes. Moth balls are necessary, but never allow the crystals to come in contact with the fabric.

• Always roll coverlets to prevent edge damage from being stored while folded. The wool and cotton or linen will weaken and break at the fold line if left for any length of time. If not using boxes for storage, place the rolled coverlet in a well-laundered pillow case or rolled in an old sheet. Be sure the sheet or pillow case has been rinsed well to remove all residue of detergent.

• *Never* store in plastic; it will hold moisture and cause mildew. Never store in an attic because of the intense summer heat, and never store in the basement because of the chance of moisture and mildew.

• Never store on a wooden shelf. Wood contains acids which will damage textiles. Always pad the shelf well with fabric or layers of acid-free tissue.

• Acid-free textile storage boxes are recommended, not only for safety but for convenience. Rolled textiles placed in the box will not be under pressure from being stacked together. The box is a convenient size to place on a shelf or tuck under a bed if storage space is limited.

Acid-free textile storage boxes and tissue may be ordered from:

University Products, Inc.
P. O. Box 101
Holyoke, MA 01041
Phone: (413) 532-3372
or (413) 532-9431

Talas
104 Fifth Avenue
New York, NY 10010

DISPLAYING YOUR COVERLETS

Coverlets were made to be utilitarian as well as decorative when the usual cottage had many people living in a small space. Beds were the major focus of the furnishings and filled up much of that space. Coverlets helped answer the desire for beauty by day, as well as furnish a warm bedcovering by night. We can still enjoy the beauty of coverlets by displaying them in our homes and using them as art objects instead of necessities. Below are a few suggestions for living with them:

• If you have a twentieth-century hand-woven coverlet, chances are it is still in good strong condition and may be used on a bed or snuggled with on a lounge.

• Coverlets may be hung on a wall if mounted properly. Use a simple sleeve stitched through on the top end so that a rod can be run through for mounting to the wall. If it does not have fringe on the bottom, a second sleeve can be stitched there and used to turn the coverlet from top to bottom several times a year; this will prevent pressure from either end while protecting the integrity of the item. If the coverlet is fragile, hand-stitch a lining of muslin or old sheeting to the back to stabilize it before sleeving. It should be at least ½" smaller than the outside overall measurements, hand-stitched in long basting stitches to protect the fragile wool.

• Velcro is easy to use for mounting. Sew a strip on the back of one end of the coverlet; glue the mating strip on a lath and fasten to the wall. Just press the top edge into place.

• Use folded on the foot of a bed or thrown over the back of a chair. If placed on a bed, be sure to remove it before using the bed. Never sit on the coverlet while it is on the bed. The pressure may break the yarn.

• Many coverlets have frayed ends from years of pulling up to chins on cold nights. These areas can just be folded under when placing on a quilt rack or thrown over a chair.

• If used as a table cover, care must be taken to protect it when food is served. Always use a glass top or a waterproof liner under a pretty linen cloth. Never allow contact with liquids—it's deadly.

• Never display in direct sunlight or reflected sunlight. Fluorescent lighting should not be used unless with an ultraviolet filter.

• Be sure to keep away from heat sources such as radiators and heat vents. And never display near an air-conditioning vent to prevent moisture and mildew.

Double Weave 68″ × 84″ Ca. 1835 United States
Two-piece. Cross motif pattern; deep blue wool and natural white cotton. Self-fringe on sides, sewn-on bottom fringe. Center seam restitched. Heavy. (*See photo 116*) VGQ/GC *$525 (D)* .... $350–$750

Double Weave 58″ × 92″ Ca. 1830–1835 United States
Two-piece. Blue, red wool, and natural white. Attached fringe on three sides. Heavy. Some losses. GQ/AC *$175 (ES)* .... $150–$350

Double Weave 72″ × 76″ Ca. 1835–1840 United States
Two-piece. Blue, rust wool, and natural white. Geometric design. Side weft fringe; top and bottom hand-hemmed. Some losses at top edge. Overall wear. GQ/AC *$275 (D)* .... $150–$350

Jacquard 85″ × 91″ Patriotic Ca. 1850 United States
One-piece. Single weave in two shades of green, two shades of brown, red wool, and natural white. Star and floral medallion center with eagles and banners "Virtue, Liberty & Independence." Borders have compotes and flowers, trees, stags, etc. Very minor stains. (*See photo 117*) VGQ/AC *$440 (A)* .... $250–$600

Jacquard 76″ × 82″ Patriotic Ca. 1876 United States
One-piece. Single weave. "Centennial, Memorial Hall, 1776–1876." Good bright colors of red, green, blue, grayish brown wool, and white. Minor wear, some very minor stains, a few small faded spots. (*See photo 118*) GQ/AC *$250 (A)* .... $150–$400

PHOTO 116

PHOTO 117

PHOTO 118

PHOTO 119

PHOTO CREDIT: GARTH'S AUCTIONS, INC.

Jacquard 68″ × 90″ 1860 Chesterville, Ohio
One-piece. Single weave. Blue and white. Four rose medallions and vintage border with eagle in one corner and "Chesterville, Ohio, 1860." The other corner marked "Manufactured Expressedly for . . . 1860." Wear and stains.
GQ/AC *$440 (A)*... $200–$600

Jacquard 78″ × 96″ 1852 Trexlertown, Pennsylvania
One-piece. Double weave. Green, red, navy blue wool, and natural white. Star and floral medallion with floral border and corners marked "Made by E. Hausman, Trexlertown, 1852." Stains. (Ephriam Hausman, ca. 1813–1901, son of Jacob, also a weaver.) (*See photo 119*) VGQ/GC *$660 (A)*........... $500–$750

The CONDITION KEY measures only the physical condition of the article and not the quality of design, materials used or workmanship.

Fine Condition (FC): As close to mint as possible; no stains or visible repairs; bright colors; no thin areas; no losses.

Good Condition (GC): Few repairs, using period threads and not obvious if repaired. All seams and hems are strong; original fringe or of the period if replaced. Colors good with slight fading of dyes; some overall wear.

Average Condition (AC): Some repairs, fading, and thinning. Minor breaks and losses. May need cleaning. This is the condition in which most are found.

Poor Condition (PC): Thinning and breaks in wool; some losses, especially at top; fading; needs cleaning. Not collectible for investment. If not valuable due to provenance, will be suitable for pillows, stuffed toys, and framed sections.

The QUALITY KEY measures the stylishness and collectibility of the piece within its category.

Good Quality (GQ): Nice piece worthy of collecting, but not for investing.

Very Good Quality (VGQ): Appealing design; good color selection; workmanship is excellent; all elements stylistically correct for period.

Superior Quality (SQ): High visual impact; expert workmanship of highest quality; all elements are superb and of the period.

PHOTO 121

PHOTO 120

Jacquard 74″ × 96″ 1842 Bethel Township, Pennsylvania
Two-piece. Single weave. Bird borders and a corner signed "Made by D.L. Myers, Bethel Township, for Elizabeth Zericel, 1842." Red, magenta, navy blue wool, natural white. One side has green stripes, the other has yellow. SQ/FC *$990 (A)*..$750–$1,200
Jacquard 82″ × 84″ Ca. 1850 United States
Two-piece. Double weave. Blue wool and white. Birds feeding young; Christian and heathen borders. Some wear. (*See photo 120*) SQ/GC *$935 (A)* ....
....$750–$1,200

> This pattern will be seen in many jacquard coverlets by many different weavers. The Christian-heathen border is very interesting, showing Boston houses and Oriental houses with palm trees.

Jacquard 78″ × 88″ Ca. 1850 United States
Two-piece. Double weave. Deep blue wool and natural white with birds feeding young. Christian and heathen border. Edge wear and stains with minor overall wear. Unsigned. GQ/GC *$500 (D)*..$300–$700
Jacquard 76″ × 84″ 1838 Morgantown, Indiana
Two-piece. Double weave. Floral design with bird border and corners signed "C.N. by D.I.G., 1838." Navy blue wool and natural white. Wear and small holes. (David Isaac Grave frequently used his initials instead of full name.) (*See photo 121*) SQ/GC *$1,107.50 (A)* ....$500–$1,200
Jacquard 74″ × 86″ 1837 Hamburg, Pennsylvania
One-piece. Single weave. Dark blue wool and natural white. Floral field with urn and bird border. Corner with "Manufactured By C. Lochman, Hamburg, PA., 1837." Provenance: Ellen Shollenberger Islett, Hamburg, Pennsylvania. (*See photo 122*) VGQ/FC *$750 (D)*....................................$500–$1,200

PHOTO 122

Overshot 72″ × 76″ Ca. 1820 United States
Natural homespun linen warp, homespun indigo wool weft. Two-part, center
seam restitched; top and bottom rehemmed; wear to wool; linen breaking. Clean.
(*See photo 123*) GQ/PC $100 (ES)..$50–$250

> This is a very early example and worthy of collecting, but not for investment
> because of the condition. Usually only the very early coverlets had homespun
> linen warps. I, personally, would not convert this into bunny rabbits, teddy
> bears or accent pillows!

PHOTO 123

Overshot 72″ × 84″ Ca. 1830 United States
Two-piece. Blue and red wool, and natural white cotton. End fringe original, side fringe has been added and could be easily removed. Optical-type pattern. GQ/AC *$198 (A)* .... $150–$350

Overshot 85″ × 90″ Ca. 1830–1835 United States
Two-piece. Optical illusion pattern in red and black wool, and white cotton. GQ/AC *$220 (A)* .... $150–$350

Overshot 64″ × 86″ Ca. 1830–1835 United States
Two-piece. Red wool and natural white with sewn-on fringe. GQ/AC *$165 (A)* .... $150–$350

Overshot 66″ × 82″ Ca. 1830 United States
Two-piece. Two shades of blue wool and natural white cotton. Self-fringe on sides; top and bottom hemmed. Some losses to top edge. GQ/GC *$325 (D)* ... . $250–$500

Overshot 70″ × 78″ Ca. 1840 United States
Two-piece. Burgundy wool and homespun linen. No fringe, rehemmed all four sides after losses. Fading in areas of burgundy wool. Simple block design. GQ/AC *$190 (D)* .... $150–$300

Summer/Winter 70″ × 90″ Ca. 1840 United States
Two-piece. Rust, black, gold wool, and natural white. Weft fringe on two sides; sewn-on fringe on bottom. Good colors; darker on side not exposed to camera. Center seam needs restitching.(*See photo 124*) VGQ/GC *$350 (D)*. $250–$500

Notice that the color pattern in the bottom fringe does not correspond with that in the coverlet. This was frequently done when the fringe was woven separately from the body, even though the same colors were used.

Summer/Winter 66″ × 84″ Ca. 1840 United States
Two-piece. Blue and white geometric design in field, wavy stripes in border. Dark blue fringe on sides; white weft fringe on bottom; top hemmed. Some wear. GQ/AC *$275 (A)* .... $150–$350

Summer/Winter 74″ × 86″ Ca. 1840 United States
Two-piece. Blue, deep red wool, and natural white. Simple geometric design. Weft fringe on sides, natural white warp fringe on bottom. Overall wear. GQ/AC *$250 (D)* .... $150–$350

PHOTO 124

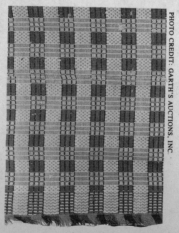

PHOTO CREDIT: GARTH'S AUCTIONS, INC.

MUSEUMS

When planning a visit to a museum, be sure to call ahead and check the days and hours which they are open to the public. Some may be open only by appointment for individual inspection and some only by appointment for guided tours to view your special interest. Museums do not keep everything on view; most displays are on a rotating schedule. It is recommended that you check their schedule before making a special trip.

There are many fine museums around the country—too many to list here. Those listed are just a sampling and suggestion for your further research.

Abby Aldrich Rockefeller Folk Art Center
Williamsburg, VA

Bayou Bend Collection
Houston, TX

Cincinnati Art Museum
Cincinnati, OH

Daughters of American Revolution (DAR) Museum
Washington, DC

Greenfield Village and Henry Ford Museum
Dearborn, MI

Henry Francis Du Pont Winterthur Museum
Winterthur, DE

Historical Society of Berks County
Reading, PA

Metropolitan Museum of Art
New York, NY

National Museum of History and Technology
Smithsonian Institution
Washington, DC

Philadelphia Museum of Art
Philadelphia, PA

The Valentine Museum
Richmond, VA

BIBLIOGRAPHY

Bishop, Robert, William Secord, and Judith Reiter Weissman. *Quilts, Coverlets, Rugs & Samplers*. New York: Alfred A. Knopf (The Knopf Collectors' Guides), 1982. A good reference for the beginner as well as the long-time collector. Full color. Handy pocket size.

Burnham, Harold B. and Dorothy K. *"Keep Me Warm One Night": Early Handweaving in Eastern Canada*. Toronto and Buffalo: Toronto Press with the Royal Museum, 1972.

Hall, Eliza Calvert. *A Book of Handwoven Coverlets*. New York: Little, Brown, and Co., 1912 (1925 edition).

Heisey, John W. *Checklist of American Coverlet Weavers*. Williamsburg, Virginia: Colonial Williamsburg Foundation, 1978 (second printing 1980). A listing of all known working weavers of the period, with a synopsis of their life and times. Very necessary if you plan to collect or own coverlets. Well illustrated.

Safford, Carleton L. and Robert Bishop. *America's Quilts and Coverlets*. New York: E.P. Dutton & Co., Inc., 1972. A good reference. Well illustrated.

Rugs

HISTORY

Early in this country's history, floors in most homes were kept bare. The only covering, for both rich and poor, was sand spread on the floors. It was swept smooth and then swirled into patterns which certainly did not last long under normal family traffic. Some simply painted the floor in various patterns, copying imported rugs or creating their own designs in stripes, geometrics or using a solid color.

The earliest rugs made in this country in the early eighteenth century were for the bed. The bed was considered the most important piece of furniture in the home, and if the housewife had time for hand-work other than necessities, she decorated the bed. These rugs were works of art and required countless hours of preparing the wool for dyeing, spinning, and weaving the fabric, and spinning the embroidery yarns. The designs were usually very simple and naive—hand-sketched flowers and animals. Most had names or initials and dates worked into the design which have greatly assisted with research and establishing provenance. By 1820, carpets and straw mats were being imported, but these were afforded only by the most affluent.

By 1830, American manufactured rugs became available, and it became fashionable to cover the floors. Most small rugs were made at home or by itinerant weavers. These small rugs were made to protect the carpet from sparks and coals from the fireplace. Hearth rugs became very popular and gave the housewife an outlet for expressing her talents. As straw matting became available, it was used extensively in the summer when there were no fires in the fireplace and in upper bedrooms year-round where there were no fireplaces. Hearth rugs were used on the hearth during the summer, over the straw matting, as a decorative touch. Rug making was a wintertime occupation, just as weaving, done when there were not as many outside chores to do and when the canning and preserving had been completed and stored.

YARN-SEWN RUGS

Most yarn-sewn rugs were made between 1800 and 1840. Unfortunately, not many were dated, as were the bed rugs. These rugs are rare and you will probably never have the joy of finding one on the market. Besides being fragile, they were used and many caught fire. They became soiled from ashes and soot or wore out from being trampled on as people gathered around the fire.

Yarn-sewn rugs were constructed with two-ply yarn on a homespun linen backing or a tow grain sack. The design was sketched on the base fabric with charcoal and a looped running stitch was used to fill in the design. The stitch was made by sewing the yarn through the base, leaving a loop on the top surface. The height of the loop was controlled sometimes with a reed or a stick. Occasionally, a yarn-sewn rug may be referred to as "reed-stitched." Many adept needleworkers were able to make the loops simply by feel and did not have to depend on the reed or stick. Many rugs had the loops clipped to form a soft pile surface. In some rugs, a portion was clipped and some was left unclipped to accent a design. The reverse of the base fabric will show flat running stitches with much of the fabric visible.

Patterns used included patriotic and nautical themes, as well as fantastic and bold animals, flowers of all sorts, and geometrics—whatever fanciful imagination the rug maker chose to indulge in. Many consider them the most beautiful pictorial rugs made in the United States.

SHIRRED RUGS

There were several types of shirred rugs: caterpillar, bias shirring, pleated shirring, and "ravel-pile." These are of appliqué-type construction; the strips are not pulled through the base fabric, which could be linen, cotton or tow grain bag.

The first, *shirred caterpillar*, was made by cutting strips of fabric one-half inch to one-and-one-half inches wide. The strips were folded in half and a running stitch was sewn along the bottom edges. The thread was then pulled to create a ruffle about three to four inches long which was sewn to the base cloth in short pieces which resembled caterpillars. They were stitched close together to fill the design and to cover the base. The surface had a close pile created by the folded, round top edges of the shirring. The reverse had only the stitched threads showing.

Bias shirring was made by cutting strips of fabric on the bias, folding them down the center, and stitching the folded bottom edge to the base fabric close to the previous strip. This created a cut pile. Only the stitching thread was visible on the reverse.

Pleated shirring was not used very often. It was constructed by cutting fabric into strips; the strips were folded into narrow pleats and each pleat was stitched individually to the fabric. The reverse showed only the running stitched thread. This method was very time consuming but made very attractive, tailored-looking graphic designs. Since this type of shirring did not lend itself well to curves, often caterpillar shirring was used in conjunction with pleating to create flowers, leaves, stems, and any other formed areas. Very few of these exist outside of museums or private collections.

The *ravel-pile* method of rug making seemed to be popular in the latter half of the nineteenth century into the early twentieth century. These cleverly designed rugs were constructed from cut strips of knitted fabric; the strips were folded in half and the raw edges were stitched together and then sewn closely together onto the base fabric. After the designs were completed, the tops of the folds were cut with scissors and left to ravel as the rug was used, creating a soft pile.

These methods converted sewing basket scraps of fabrics into inexpensive and colorful decorations for the floor. They remained popular until around 1850 when burlap was imported to this country. The use of burlap for hooked rugs continued to utilize scraps and discarded clothing. As you will see, hooked rugs proved to be more durable than shirred rugs and they were less time consuming to make.

HOOKED RUGS

With the importation of burlap into this country around 1850, hooked rugs became the popular method of construction. Burlap is a sturdy material made from jute or hemp. It found its way to America from India via England, Scotland, and Ireland, where the coarse fabric was manufactured. It was mostly used for feed sacks, and the enterprising housewife immediately recognized it as a new material to be utilized in rug making; it also relieved her from the weaving of tow. The sacks were ripped open, washed, and stretched. The size of the rug was determined by the size of the laundered sack. Designs were sketched on or, in many cases, the rug maker just went free-form with her design and followed the whim of the moment, guided only by her enthusiasm and the material available at hand. These are the primitive designs to be treasured and are much sought after by collectors.

Rug hooking seems to have been born in New England and eastern Canada, eventually spreading down to Pennsylvania, the South, and finally the western part of the country. Many cottage industries sprang up around the country by women who were anxious to turn their spare-time activity into a small income. One interesting cottage industry came out of Labrador. The Grenfell Mission was formed in Newfoundland, Labrador, by Dr. Wilfred Grenfell, who designed rugs to be worked by the inhabitants during the long frozen winters. This afforded subsistence during the time spent away from fishing and fur trapping. These designs were mostly of local scenes such as puffins, icebergs, houses with snowy backgrounds, polar bears, and seascapes, and were worked with whatever fabric and discarded clothing was available. The Grenfell Mission was active between 1900 and 1920. Many are labeled on the back.

Hooking was thus a new form of rug making in the late nineteenth century, using a hook to pull narrow strips of fabric up through the holes in the burlap. Burlap was a simple weave having regular openings in the warp and weft which made hooking easy to achieve. This was impossible with close-woven linen or wool. The hook was also a very simple implement, made at home from the carpenter's work box. The rug hook was made from an ordinary nail—the nail head was flattened and inserted into a wooden handle, and the point was turned up into a hook. Nothing could have been simpler or less expensive, especially to achieve such widespread use and produce so many beautiful pieces of floor coverings. The important thing was that the housewife could use the material in her sewing basket as well as discarded clothing. Even though manufactured cotton fabrics were relatively easy to obtain and inexpensive, they were still out of the realm of affordability of the thrifty housewife who could not afford new fabrics for her rugs. And she liked the idea that she could produce these rugs for her home with what she had available. The original hooked rug was *not* made with yarns—it was made with narrow strips of fabrics. The fabric was usually cut one-quarter-inch wide if using wool. If thinner fabrics were used, such as mixing cotton or linen with wool in the same rug, these were cut wider and folded to one-quarter-inch width to maintain the same thickness and weight of pattern in the rug. The diversity of fabrics used made for some very interesting textures in the patterns and motifs. Even though hooked rugs were considered a form of relaxation, it was still labor intensive—the fabrics had to be cut into strips and dyed at home to produce desired colors; the base burlap had to be prepared; a design had to be developed and sketched; and then hours were spent hooking and finishing the end product.

What we consider folk art today was not regarded as such in the nineteenth century. None of the fashionable ladies' magazines or needlework journals mentioned very much about rug hooking—it was considered a cabin craft and beneath notice of proper Victorians. They did, however, run ads for patterns and other necessary materials. Because hooked rugs were not regarded as an art form, very few exist today that are older than the late 1890s or early twentieth century. As they wore thin they were relegated to the dog basket or used as mud rugs outside doorways. Many were used to pad furniture in moving—one of the primary reasons why so many quilts and coverlets have met their fate.

A Maine tin peddler, Edward Sands Frost, had a great influence on the designs of hooked rugs in the latter half of the nineteenth century. He cut tin patterns and stencils which he used to stamp burlap to be made into rugs. This grew into the profitable business of furnishing pre-printed and colored burlap, which he peddled to housewives on his regular route. His designs were usually stiffly posed animals with bold flowers and geometric motifs inside borders. These finally were advertised widely. Following Frost were pre-printed patterns advertised by the Diamond Dye Co. and Montgomery Ward Co., among others. Many of these rugs have an individual look to them because the rug maker used her own choice of colors and fabrics in completing the designs, and also frequently missed the outlines of the patterns by modifying them to her own taste.

Rug hooking remained popular into the early twentieth century and then saw a renewed interest in the 1920s and 1930s with the revival of American colonial decor. Although hooked rugs were not from the eighteenth century, they seemed to blend well with the simple styles of furnishings and the soft wood tones used in furniture of that era and thus were quickly adopted as "colonial."

WOVEN RUGS

Woven rugs were made from the early days of the colonial period up to the nineteenth century. These rugs were made of cotton on the hand loom. The width of the strips was determined by the width of the loom. Most were in striped designs made by adding colored weft yarns. Room sizes were achieved by sewing these strips together at the side edges. Many early paintings, done by itinerant artists in this country, show brightly colored striped carpets on the floors, and the artists documented them in almost painful reproduction. Because of these paintings, reproductions of these rugs are now available from several major folk art retail firms. They are in documented designs and colors in order to fill the market demand for period-style floor coverings.

In the nineteenth century, housewives made woven rugs on simple wooden hand looms from dyed cotton fabric remnants and discarded clothing. These were a bright mixture of colors and fabrics, and were unlike the hand-loomed cotton rugs mentioned above. They are often referred to as "rag rugs." Many women made these for market to add to their income, including the Amish and Shakers.

BRAIDED RUGS

Braided rugs date from about 1830, and these were also made from scrap fabrics and discarded clothing. Long narrow strips were cut and braided together and then laid flat and formed into a circle; the edges were stitched together with strong thread and a stout needle to complete the rug. The thickness of the rug was determined by the thickness of the braid, which was determined by the width of each strip of fabric used in the braid. It was important to use all materials of the same weight to achieve a rug of even thickness—wool with wool, cotton with cotton. Early braided rugs were a wonderful mish-mash of color and random pattern, but soon the rug maker learned how to plan and arrange patterns of colors in the braids. This type of rug was a joy to the housewife because it was less labor intensive and no designing skills were required; they just happily braided away and let the design fall where it may! The Shakers were considered the finest braided rug makers. They planned ingenious color schemes and laid them out into concentric circles which made very attractive and interesting rugs. They are highly collectible today, if you are lucky enough to find one.

Braided rugs made a renewed appearance in the 1920s and 1930s when they were considered a proper accent for American colonial revival style.

PENNY RUGS

These wonderful rugs are of appliquéd construction dating from the late nineteenth to the early twentieth century. The *penny* is cut from wool or felt and appliquéd onto a base fabric, usually linen or some other heavy material. A blanket stitch or other similar stitch decorated the outside edge of each round. Some will show smaller "coins" appliquéd to the top of each penny. It is thought the term "penny" was derived from the early nineteenth-century coin that may have been used as a pattern, originally, for cutting the rounds. These still show up occasionally at antiques shows and in shops.

COLLECTING TIPS

- The most important thing to check is *condition*. If the foundation is dry, brittle or cracking, the rug will not be collectible for investment or use.
- A rug with a brittle foundation will be too expensive to have repaired—or may not be repairable at all.
- Visual impact is important. Consider *originality* of design and good use of fabrics and colors within the design. Some rugs with expert workmanship and stunning visual impact may be more valuable than older rugs without that indefinable *something*, which is charm.
- You cannot judge the age of a rug by the use of fabrics alone. Many women used worn clothing and fabrics which they had collected for years before making their rugs.
- Check the foundation material. Early makers used linen, tow or wool for the base. Burlap was imported to this country around 1850. If the rug has a burlap backing, it cannot be earlier than 1850. However, some rug makers used linen past the 1850 date, so check for the types of fabrics and dyes used if the base is not burlap.
- The hooked rugs that we see today date from the middle of the nineteenth century, along with the introduction of burlap.
- Style of pattern is not a true indication of age; many designs used in the early 1930s were copied from earlier motifs and prints. Check the type of fabrics and dyes used.
- Dates which are woven in the rug may not be a reliable indication of age. Many were made to celebrate a personal anniversary or special event. Some were made as a commemorative or political token.
- Always check the back of a rug for the marks of a pattern which may have been printed. Many show the name of the pattern, stock number, and colors and types of yarns to be used. Also, it may show a crudely sketched original design.

Remember: No rug is older than the youngest element
in the original construction.

QUALITY AND CONDITION KEYS

CONDITION KEYS

Measures only the physical condition of the article and not the quality of design, material or workmanship.

Fine Condition (FC): As near mint as possible. The most important consideration in rug condition is the backing. The backing must not be brittle, whether burlap, linen, tow or wool. Edges intact; colors are correct for age and mellowed properly. Minor repairs executed in a professional manner and not obvious on face of rug. No thin areas. No moth damage to wool rugs. Clean.

Good Condition (GC): Few repairs that are not too obvious; fabrics and colors have aged properly for age. Edges intact; no stains; no thin areas. Clean.

Average Condition (AC): Some repairs, minor fading, slight thinning; minor spots; may need cleaning or repairs. This is the condition in which rugs are most often found.

Poor Condition (PC): Brittleness to foundation; some rips or tears; losses; fading. Needs cleaning. Not worthy of collecting or investment. May be useful as example or for pattern.

QUALITY KEYS

Measures the stylishness and collectibility of the piece within its category.

Good Quality (GQ): Attractive piece worthy of collecting, but not for investment.

Very Good Quality (VGQ): Visually attractive; colors and design well defined; well executed; all elements stylistically correct for period.

Superior Quality (SQ): Artistically stunning; design well executed; expert workmanship; all elements are superb and of the period.

MARKET TRENDS

Handmade rugs are considered an American folk art form and are highly collectible. They are a visual delight and important in the antiques, collectible, and decorating field. They blend well with any period and any style, especially the relaxed, informal country look that is so popular at this time. Since the late 1960s and early 1970s, renewed interest in collecting these marvelous textiles has skyrocketed. Needless to say, prices have kept pace with the interest in collecting. Many rugs may still be purchased for a few hundred dollars, and the finer, more original designs can range upwards of several thousand dollars. Major considerations are condition, eye appeal, workmanship, and originality of design.

The market is still active; values are constantly appreciating and probably will continue for the finer, more attractive rugs.

CARING FOR
YOUR RUGS

Rugs should be treated with the special care they deserve as pieces of folk art. Many are old and fragile, and many contain fabrics or yarns which have been home-dyed and will not withstand vigorous cleaning or washing. My first suggestion when handling antique, heirloom or valuable textiles is to consult an expert conservator/restorationist for an evaluation of age and condition, and for advice on how best to approach cleaning. Here are a few suggestions which may be helpful:

• First, *never* put your rug in a washing machine, no matter how delicate the cycle may be.

• Never vacuum directly on the surface of the fabric, front or back. Use the same system as with antique quilts; lay the rug flat on the floor and cover completely with a layer of cheesecloth that is a few inches wider all around. Weight the cheesecloth down around its edges and then use the low-suction control, holding the nozzle an inch or so above the surface. Turn the rug over and repeat on the other side.

• Sometimes a soft brush will suffice in removing dust from the surface, back or front.

• *Never* shake or beat a rug. This violent motion will shred the backing and cause splitting or tears.

• If you feel that you must clean or launder the rug, test the dyes first. Use a white cloth with plain water and sponge a small spot of *each* color. If it smudges the cloth it is not colorfast. Check the foundation as well. If it is burlap and was not laundered before using it, it will show a rusty yellow stain. If you have determined that the dyes will not run, proceed with a soft cloth or brush dipped in tepid water with a mild cleansing agent; sponge a small area at a time and then rinse well with plain water. Just surface clean; do not let the entire rug become wet to the foundation.

• I have found that the easiest way to launder a colorfast newer rug, when necessary, is to float it in the bath tub in cool water with a mild detergent. Pat it gently or brush with a soft brush. Let the water out and rinse several times without handling the rug. When the tub is empty of water, pat the rug to remove as much water as possible. Handle the wet rug with great care; the bulk of weight from the water may cause splitting or tearing. Pick the whole wet mass up in one bundle and roll in a heavy bath towel to remove excess water. Always roll the rug with the top outside. Lay the rug flat to dry; if outside, be sure it is out of direct sunlight. *Do not twist or wring*.

• Never hang a rug on the line or over a hanger; the weight will cause damage or a permanent crease.

• When storing, never use plastic. Plastic will hold in moisture and cause mildew or rotting. Also, as with all textiles, never store in an attic or basement because of the possibility of dampness and/or extreme heat. Extreme heat will dry out the foundation and cause brittleness.

• The safest way to store is to roll, top side out, on a padded, acid-free roller; sleeve with an old piece of sheeting to keep out dust. Be sure the sheet or fabric covering has been rinsed well to remove all residue of detergent to prevent fading or damage to the rug. Stand the roller in the corner of a closet where you store your finest clothing!

• The roller may be a tube from the fabric shop or a wooden dowel. Be sure to pad, because wood and cardboard contain acids which will cause damage.

• If storing with moth balls, never allow them to come in contact with the rug to prevent damage.

Remember: When in doubt, consult an expert!

DISPLAYING
YOUR RUGS

Many of the antique rugs handed down to us today probably were prized examples of the housewife's artistic talents and kept for show, used on a table top or kept stored away in a hope chest. That's why some of them are still with us! However, today we would like to be able to use them in the decor of our rooms where they can not only make a statement but afford visual enjoyment as well. Old soft-hued rugs add such warmth and personality to a room. They may be thrown over a table top, used on the floor away from any traffic pattern, draped over the back of a chair or thrown across the foot of a bed as you would a quilt.

Following are a few hints for displaying your rugs:

• The best way to hang a rug is to stitch a fabric backing about three to five inches larger than the dimensions of the rug. Stitch into the binding on the edges, not into the face of the rug. Treat a piece of board approximately one-half inch smaller than the rug or cover with padding to protect the backing fabric from the acids in the wood. Turn the protruding edges to the back of the board and staple on or use tacks. It may then be hung as you would a painting with no stress to the rug.

• Never display a rug near a source of heat or air-conditioning. The moisture and heat will cause mildew.

• Do not display rugs in direct sunlight or artificial lighting; this will cause fading.

• If using on the floor, be sure to place it out of the traffic pattern where it can be enjoyed, but not trod upon.

RUGS LISTING

All rugs listed are worked on burlap unless otherwise noted.

Braided Cotton 35″ × 37″ Ca. 1940 United States
Unusual form, made from seven braided rounds, 12″ dia. each, stitched together. Faded pink, green, and black. Some wear. GQ/AC *$42.50 (A)* ....
.... $25–$50

Braided Rag 36″ × 50″ Ca. 1950 Southern United States
Well designed with areas of color and print; light and dark fabrics. Multicolors with blues predominating. *(See photo 125)* GQ/FC *$195 (D)* .... $150–$250

Braided Wool 32″ × 54″ Ca. 1940 Pennsylvania
Solid shades of dark plum, rose, beige, deep rose, and navy wool. Well designed in rings of shaded colors. *(See photo 126)* VGQ/GC *$335 (D)* ...... $250–$400

Crocheted Rag 25″ × 50″ Ca. 1950 Southern United States
Oval crocheted cotton rag strips. Multicolor including blue, yellow, orange, and gray. GQ/AC *$25 (ES)* .... $10–$50

Grospoint 20″ × 40″ Ca. 1950 United States
Handmade with wool. Four stitches to the inch. Very bright and rich colors of red, blue, gold, purple, and black. Canvas is splitting. *(See photo 127)* GQ/
PC *$35 (ES)* .... $25–$50

Hooked Rag 26″ × 103″ runner Ca. 1900–1910 United States
Geometric star design in good old colors. Minor wear. GQ/GC *$550 (A)* ......
.... $400–$750

Hooked Rag 40½″ × 58″ Ca. 1920–1930 United States
Colorful stripes in alternating squares, basketweave style. Striped border. Unused condition. GQ/FC *$385 (A)* .... $250–$500

Hooked Rag 33″ × 72″ Ca. 1950 United States
Stripes in vivid solid colors. Binding has some wear. GQ/AC *$330 (A)* ....
.... $250–$500

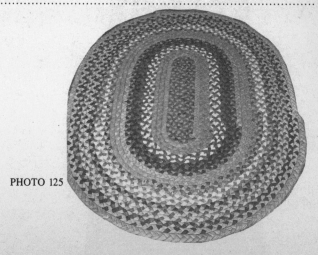

PHOTO 125

PHOTO 126

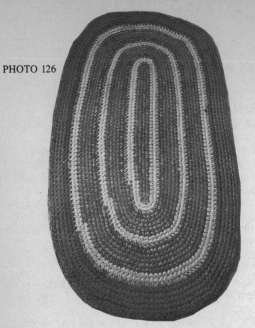

PHOTO 127

The CONDITION KEY measures only the physical condition of the article and not the quality of design, material or workmanship.

Fine Condition (FC): As near mint as possible. The most important consideration in rug condition is the backing. The backing must not be brittle, whether burlap, linen, tow or wool. Edges intact; colors are correct for age and mellowed properly. Minor repairs executed in a professional manner and not obvious on face of rug. No thin areas. No moth damage to wool rugs. Clean.

Good Condition (GC): Few repairs that are not too obvious; fabrics and colors have aged properly for age. Edges intact; no stains; no thin areas. Clean.

Average Condition (AC): Some repairs, minor fading, slight thinning; minor spots; may need cleaning or repairs. This is the condition in which rugs are most often found.

Poor Condition (PC): Brittleness to foundation; some rips or tears; losses; fading. Needs cleaning. Not worthy of collecting or investment. May be useful as example or for pattern.

The QUALITY KEY measures the stylishness and collectibility of the piece within its category.

Good Quality (GQ): Attractive piece worthy of collecting, but not for investment.

Very Good Quality (VGQ): Visually attractive; colors and design well defined; well executed; all elements stylistically correct for period.

Superior Quality (SQ): Artistically stunning; design well executed; expert workmanship; all elements are superb and of the period.

Hooked Rag 24½″ × 47″   Ca. 1900   United States
Primitive; gray cat with ball on a green stripe ground with black, maroon, pink, and rose. Damage; repair necessary along one side. *(See photo 128)* GQ/PC *$302.50 (A)* .... $250–$500

Hooked Rag 36″ × 66″   Ca. 1920   United States
Horse and buggy, dog and flying goose all in dark blue silhouetted against an oval light blue sky with clouds. Border design in brown and other colors. Signed in corner. Minor wear. *(See photo 129)* GQ/AC *$550 (A)* .... $350–$750

This appears to be a take-off on the old-time doctor trying to beat the stork! The subject of many silhouettes.

PHOTO 128

PHOTO CREDIT: GARTH'S AUCTIONS, INC.

PHOTO 129

Hooked Rag   17½″ × 34″   Ca. 1900   United States
Good folk art scene with black horse in stylized silhouette on a greenish ground with brown border. Man in various shades of brown, black, and red. Minor wear and a few stitches missing. Unusual crocheted brown yarn edge. *(See photo 130)* VGQ/GC *$1,045 (A)* .... $850–$1,200

Hooked Rag   31″ × 53″   Ca. 1890–1900   United States
Running horse in several shades of red on a dark ground. Stylized plants and stump, segmented border in reds and browns. Some wear and edge damage. Good color. The horse fills the field; fine folk art rendition. VGQ/AC *$1,760 (A)*... $1,500–$2,000

Hooked Rag   24″ × 37″   Ca. 1930   United States
Airedale with colorful background; dark border. Worn and some areas are missing. Apparently from a pattern. GQ/PC *$125 (D)* ....$50–$250

Hooked Rag   20″ × 36½″   Ca. 1930–1940   United States
Two brown puppies on green grass with a yellow picket fence, blue bowl, and red border. Black outlines. Minor wear. GQ/AC *$247.50 (A)*....... $150–$350

Hooked Rag   25″ × 35″   Ca. 1920   United States
Original. Stylized landscape with house, trees, birds, flowers, etc. Colors have faded to a pleasant blend of pale blues, grays, and greenish gray with white, black, and pink. Mounted on a stretcher as a wall hanging. Very charming. VGQ/GC *$495 (A)*... $350–$600

PHOTO 130

Hooked Rag 24″ × 35½″ Ca. 1930 Maine
Well-detailed scene of the Nubble Island Lighthouse, Maine, by Josephine
Moulton Bartlett, Eliot, Maine. Hand-dyed wool has a good graduation of
shading of colors. Hooked inscription in lower right reads "The Nubble."
(One of a series of lighthouses printed on burlap.) VGQ/FC *$385 (A)* ....
.... $250–$500

Hooked Rag 27″ × 72″ Ca. 1950–1960 United States
Penny design in many colors and various sizes scattered on a gray striated ground.
With colorful striped border. Unused condition. VGQ/FC *$1,292 (A)* ....
.... $1,000–$1,850

Hooked Rag 79″ × 112″ Ca. 1970 United States
Very colorful stylized leaf design with a bluish gray stripe design ground. Unused condition. VGQ/FC *$2,860 (A)* .... $2,500–$3,500

Hooked Rag 27½″ × 39½″ Ca. 1910 Canada
Grenfell type. Reindeer-pulled rescue sled with two figures in a winter landscape. Some fading and with little edge damage. VGQ/AC *$495 (A)* ....
.... $350–$600

Hooked Rag and Yarn 24″ × 41″ Ca. 1930 United States
Bird on a branch with good colors, on a beige ground. Wear; some repair necessary. GQ/AC *$220 (A)* .... $150–$300

Hooked Rag and Yarn 31″ × 46″ Ca. 1930 United States
Two blue parrots in polychrome floral design on a beige ground with browns,
salmon, and black. Minor wear. VGQ/AC *$550 (A)* .... $350–$650

Hooked Wool 27″ × 46″ 1970 Yardley, Pennsylvania
Home-dyed wool with natural dyes. Crewel-designed "Kensington" pattern by
Pearl McGown. Ivory field; rose, yellow, and blue flowers. Signed lower edge
"C.T.Z., 1970." *(See photo 131)* VGQ/FC *Value $450 (Private Collection)*

Pearl McGown, a famous teacher of rug hooking, founded the National Guild
of Pearl McGown, Inc. It was the first rug-hooking guild in the United States
and is still active in teaching traditional methods of dyeing and hooking. This
rug was made by Camille T. Zagaroli, a guild member, who also dyed the
wool fabric with homemade vegetable dyes.

Hooked Wool 24″ × 36″ 1980 Pennsylvania
Wool fabric home-dyed with Putnam dyes. White cat, "Frank," with one blue
and one green eye. Blue field with gray dentil motif border. A Jane McGown
Flynn-designed "Cat Mat." Worked by Alma Coia, a teacher and member of
the National Guild of Pearl McGown, Inc. *(See photo 132)* SQ/FC *Value $500
(Private Collection)*...

Hooked Yarn 27″ × 71″ Ca. 1910–1920 Eastern Pennsylvania
Wool yarn in geometric pattern. In colors of black, red, and mixed colored
stripes. Bright colors. One minor tear. *(See photo 133)* VGQ/GC *$425 (D)* ....
.... $350–$500

Hooked Yarn 22″ × 30″ Ca. 1910–1920 Pennsylvania
Wool yarn. Multicolor striped center, multicolor blocks in border. Bright colors.
(See photo 134) GQ/GC *$150 (D)* .... $50–$200

Hooked Yarn 22½″ × 32″ Ca. 1920–1930 Eastern Pennsylvania
Wool yarn. Multicolor stripes, dark blue and off-white end border. Good colors.
One break on edge. *(See photo 135)* GQ/AC *$95 (D)* .... $50–$125

PHOTO 131

PHOTO 132

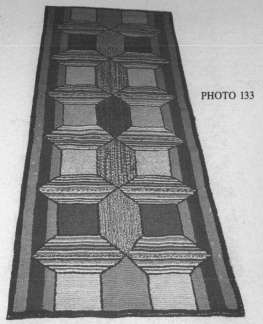

PHOTO 133

PHOTO 134

PHOTO 135

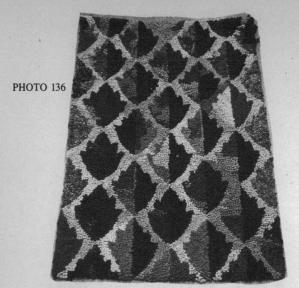

PHOTO 136

PHOTO 137

PHOTO 138

Hooked Yarn 22″ × 36″ Ca. 1940 United States
Wool yarn. All-over stylized leaf design in shades of wine, mauve, burgundy, and gray. From a kit. Burlap dry. *(See photo 136)* GQ/PC *$25 (D)* ... $10–$35

Hooked Yarn 48″ × 72″ Ca. 1930 Alamance County, North Carolina
Wool yarn. Square motifs outlined with oak leaves, centers of flowers and squares with block designs. In fall colors of beige, tan, yellows, oranges, and brown border. From a kit. Colors mellowed to soft tones. *(See photo 137)* VGQ/ GC *$525 (D)* .... $450–$650

Hooked Yarn 38″ × 42″ Ca. 1900–1910 United States
Wool yarn. Center motif of deep red flower and green shamrocks on cream ground; brown boughs with tan leaves; border of black that is fading to browns. Edge wear; tear needing repair. *(See photo 138)* VGQ/PC *$125 (D)* ....
.... $100–$200

A visually stunning rug, but low value due to condition.

Hooked Yarn 27″ × 40″ Ca. 1940 Coastal New Jersey
Wool yarn. Mauve center; mauve and rose-shaded flower in each corner on black border. Back stamped with "Modern," design P952, and information for required yarn colors. *(See photo 139)* GQ/FC *$350 (D)* .... $250–$400

Hooked Yarn 23″ × 42″ Ca. 1930 China
Wool yarn. Pastel flowers in leafy cartouche, pale blue ground, dark brown border. *(See photo 140)* GQ/GC *$135 (D)* .... $100–$200

Hooked Yarn 24″ × 36″ Ca. 1930–1940 New England
Wool yarn. Worked in various shades of yellow, gold, and mustard with black border. For accent, some of the pile is clipped and some left looped. From a kit. *(See photo 141)* GQ/GC *$325 (D)* .... $250–$450

Hooked Yarn 18″ × 36″ 1956 Burlington, New Jersey
Wool yarn. Designed specifically as a gift to a new homeowner: Washington Monument, street sign, house on hill, the heart in the home, hand, etc. Bright shades of red, royal blue, marigold yellow, purple, and black. Designed and worked by Jane Williams. *(See photo 142)* VGQ/FC *$500 (D)* ...... $400–$600

PHOTO 139

PHOTO 140

PHOTO 141

PHOTO 142

PHOTO 143

Hooked Yarn   22″ × 44″   Ca. 1940   United States
Wool yarn. Demilune hearth rug. Gray striated field with violet and purple flowers, green leaves, and green border. From a kit. *(See photo 143)* GQ/AC   *$75 (D)* .... $50–$150
Hooked Yarn   24″ × 48″   Ca. 1930–1940   United States
Wool yarn. Demilune hearth rug. ''Welcome'' in black on a beige field, surrounded by pastel flowers, black border. GQ/FC   *$125 (D)* .... $50–$150
Hooked Yarn   22″ × 50″   Ca. 1940–1950   United States
Wool yarn. All-over design of small blocks in colors of beige, tan, brown, gold, and black. Black and tan border. Clipped pile. Damage to edges. All-over wear, limp. *(See photo 144)* GQ/AC   *$75 (D)* .... $25–$100
Hooked Yarn   20″ × 32½″   Ca. 1930   United States
Wool yarn. Silhouette of black cat on a pillow with multicolored ''bubbles'' background. Wear and colors faded. Rebacked and some small repairs. *(See photo 145)* GQ/PC   *$215 (A)* .... $150–$300
Hooked Yarn   32″ × 32″   Ca. 1940–1950   United States
Wool yarn. Stylized rooster, bright colors, on a salmon ground. *(See photo 146)* GQ/VGC   *$330 (A)* .... $200–$400

PHOTO 144

PHOTO 145

PHOTO 146

PHOTO 147

PHOTO 148

Hooked Yarn and Braided 20″ × 30″ Ca. 1920–1930 Maine
Wool yarn and wool braided. Lighthouse design with house in background, ocean waves in foreground. Shades of blue, green, and gray. Red roof. Bordered with four rows of braided wool in shades of dark blue, beige, and black. Hooked area from a kit. *(See photo 147)* VGQ/FC *$525 (D)* .... $450–$600

Hooked Yarn and Knit 23″ × 38″ Ca. 1900–1920 North Carolina
Pink flowers and green leaves hooked with knitted cotton fabric. Pale blue background of wool yarn; the four corners are hooked yarn in a variety of colored blocks, each outlined in black. Colors have mellowed; edges need reworking. A very attractive original design. *(See photo 148)* GQ/PC *$150 (D)* .....$50–$250

> This is another example of an extremely attractive rug that has been undervalued because of condition.

Needlepoint 39″ × 62″ Ca. 1950 United States
Handmade with wool on canvas, five stitches to the inch. Maroon background; center of floral medallion in pastels on pink; gold ribbon bow frame. Back lined with ivory cotton sateen. Well made. *(See photo 149)* VGQ/FC *$500 (D)* ......
.... $350–$550

Penny Rug 25″ × 56″ Ca. 1900 Eastern shore, Virginia
Base of dark green heavy linen; hand-hemmed edges. Pennies of black heavy wool; each overlaid with three smaller pennies. All pennies are bound with embroidery thread in blanket stitch. Assorted bright colors in the small pennies. Colors still bright. *(See photo 150)* VGQ/AC *$225 (D)* .... $150–$350

Penny Rug 34″ × 66″ Ca. 1920 United States
Colorful diamond design in wool rectangle. Predominately black and red with other colors. Wear; fading with some loose circles. GQ/AC *$192.50 (A)* ....
.... $150–$250

Penny Rug 51½″ × 58″ Ca. 1930 Ellsworth, Maine
Six-point star shape. Wool medallions with black and shades of olive on maroon circles on an ivory-colored ground. Minor wear. GQ/GC *$440 (A)* ....
.... $300–$500

Shirred 30″ × 36″ Ca. 1920 Eastern shore, Virginia
Heavy knitted base, black wool yarn. Bias shirred in silk fabrics. Knitted black border; interior of random colors of mauve, rose, and beige. Some losses. *(See photo 151)* GQ/PC *$275 (D)* .... $150–$350

PHOTO 149

PHOTO 150

PHOTO 151

PHOTO 152

Shirred and Hooked 26″ × 42″ Ca. 1880 New England
Dog is yarn-hooked in shades of yellow and beige with underside hooked in flecked rag. Standing on tan surface with mixed colored background. Framed in rose-colored yarn. Flowers are shirred caterpillar stitch in brighter rose. Oval liner of gold. Professional repair to lower right corner. Colors mellowed softly. *(See photo 152)* VGQ/GC *$525 (D)*.................................... $450–$650

> This was a visually appealing rug. Unfortunately, it had been damaged, and this was reflected in the value.

Woven Rag 3′1″ × 15′6″ Ca. 1920–1930 Pennsylvania
Four strips. Shades of brown in weft, stripes of bright red and natural color warp. Stains and some color bleeding, minor wear. One has damage. Would make a room-size rug 12′4″ × 15′6″. GQ/PC *$1,078 Lot (A)*.................
.... $800–$1,250 Lot
Woven Rag 10′ × 14′3″ Ca. 1900–1920 Pennsylvania
Room-size rug made from four strips. Red, white, and green stripes on a light bluish-gray ground. Some wear and damage. GQ/PC *$242 (A)* ..... $150–$350
Woven Rag 3′ × 14′9″ Ca. 1900–1920 Pennsylvania
Strip. Beige with red stripes. Some wear. GQ/PC *$150 (A)* .... $100–$200
Woven Rag 33″ × 13′ Ca. 1920–1930 Zoar, Ohio
One strip. Unused and with good rich color. Random use of colors. One end bound with blue and gold homespun, the other end unbound. VGQ/FC *$330 (A)*.. $250–$450
Yarn Sewn 25″ × 43″ Nineteenth century Pennsylvania
Hand-sewn yarn shag. Bright colors in random pattern. Cotton ticking back. Attributed to Mt. Lebanon Shakers. Knit wool edge binding has damage. *(See photo 153)* GQ/AC *$93.50 (A)*... $50–$150

PHOTO 153

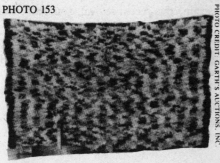

MUSEUMS AND RUG-HOOKING GUILDS

MUSEUMS

There are many museums around the country which have a permanent collection of American handmade rugs. Listed below is just a representative sampling. Always check ahead for hours, days open to public, and if appointments are necessary to view your special interest.

Beauport
Gloucester, MA

Lincoln House, Old Sturbridge Village
Sturbridge, MA

Dallas Art Museum
Dallas, TX

Museum of American Folk Art
New York, NY

Henry Ford Museum
Dearborn, MI

Shelburne Museum
Shelburne, VT

RUG-HOOKING GUILDS

There is a great interest in learning the craft of rug hooking today. For information concerning this recent revival, you may check with the guilds listed below.

Association of Traditional Hooking Artists (ATHA)
Nancy Martin
National Membership Chairman
1360 Newman Avenue
Seekonk, MA 02771

National Guild of Pearl McGown, Inc.
Jane McGown Flynn
Box 1301
Sterling, MA 01564

BIBLIOGRAPHY

Bishop, Robert, William Secord, and Judith Reiter Weissman. *Quilts, Coverlets, Rugs & Samplers*. New York: Alfred A. Knopf, 1982. An informative, handy pocket-size book; full-color illustrations.

Kopp, Joel and Kate. *American Hooked and Sewn Rugs: Art Underfoot*. New York: E.P. Dutton Co., Inc., 1985. An important reference.

Little, Nina Fletcher. *Floor Coverings in New England Before 1850*. Sturbridge, Massachusetts: Old Sturbridge Village Booklet Series, 1967.

Montgomery, Florence M. *Printed Textiles: English and American Cottons and Linens 1700–1850*. New York: A Winterthur Book/The Viking Press, 1970.

Zarbock, Barbara J. *The Complete Book of Rug Hooking*. New York: Van Nostrand Reinhold Co., 1961.

Samplers

HISTORY

One of the most sought-after examples of early American needlework is the sampler. These works of art were made by young girls, many before their teen years, to demonstrate their expertise with the needle. They show in almost painful detail their skillful training. It was considered necessary to know fancy and fine needlework in order to mark the household linens and clothing; and it was considered a social skill towards making a proper marriage. At the time, samplers were not intended to be works of art, as we now think of them, but were patterns of stitches and designs to be used later in the necessary hand-stitching all housewives were compelled to do. They were kept in a drawer or hope chest and only referred to when needed as a guide for a special stitch. They represent, for the most part, the sum of the only education many girls received in the early years of our country.

Young girls from well-to-do families were sent to schools where they were taught social graces, reading and writing, music, art, and needlework. Needlework was the most important part of their education and accomplishments in this area gave them the most pride.

MARKING SAMPLERS

Some of the earliest samplers were small and referred to as "marking samplers." These "markt" samplers displayed the alphabet and frequently numbers in fine cross stitch on homespun linen. They were used as guides for marking household linens with initials and numbers. This made it possible for the housewife to rotate linens for even use and wear. Linens made up about twenty to twenty-five percent of the entire household inventory and this was an important consideration. Most often these marking samplers were made by very young girls and were a learning exercise before undertaking the task of serious samplers. Marking samplers were usually only three to five inches deep and approximately six to eight inches wide. (See the miniature sampler, $1\frac{1}{2}'' \times 1\frac{1}{2}''$, in the Valentine Museum color section in this book!) These wonderful miniature samplers are very collectible today and make a stunning display if framed and hung in a group. Many on the market today are English. The American markt samplers may have more writing than their English cousins.

BAND SAMPLERS

During the late eighteenth century, many of the samplers were long and narrow. These were made in horizontal bands of flowers, grape clusters, and leaves in a variety of stitches, as well as of alphabets and numbers. This type of band sampler did not have a worked border and frequently had additions of bands as more stitches were learned or designs practiced. These were usually worked in silk on homespun linen.

ALPHABET SAMPLERS

In the early nineteenth century, the sampler grew shorter and wider in shape. Many of these were worked in alphabets and numbers. A typical sampler may have as many as four to six different styles of letters using different types of stitches, and several forms of numbers. The maker usually signed her name, age, and date along with simple designs such as a house with trees, presumably her home or school. Vining borders began to appear at this time as well.

VERSE SAMPLERS

These samplers began showing many more designs of flowers, strawberries, birds, potted plants, and landscapes. The most important feature was the verse which was worked with minute stitches and usually filled the center of the sampler. These verses probably came from Isaac Watt's *Divine Songs for Children*, and also from Shakespeare and the Bible. Some were written by the children themselves. Many were fatalistic, too, mentioning ''when I am in my grave, remember me''—rather gloomy by today's standards!

ALPHABET AND VERSE SAMPLERS

You will find some samplers with the alphabet, numbers, and a verse. These will show borders, flowers, vining, a house or any of the popular motifs of that time. They were made primarily in the early to mid-nineteenth century.

FAMILY RECORD SAMPLERS

This type of sampler was made in England as well as America. It shows the names of the parents, their birth and marriage dates, and all of the children's names with birth dates and frequently death dates. One popular design is an arch above two pillars with the listing in the center;

vines, flowers, and usually green grass and flowers appear at the base. Sometimes there is a house, a church, and trees. The young maker signed her name and date of completion. Many family record samplers will also show alphabets and numbers.

PICTORIAL SAMPLERS

These samplers show so much charm and originality because the young people who made them filled up most of the open space with things that fascinated or pleased them. Some depict a scene from a biblical story, favorite animals, flowers, urns, vining borders, homes or schools, and sometimes adults which represent parents. These are signed and dated, and frequently show the name of the school mistress.

MAP SAMPLERS

Map samplers were popular in England as well as America. American map samplers may be dated back to 1775. Many of these samplers do not show the workmanship of other, more highly designed pieces and do not use a great variety of stitches. It may seem that this was one way of making a sampler and not having to spend as many hours laboring over it—the lazy girl's way out! However, American map samplers are rare and should be considered when collecting.

MOURNING SAMPLERS

With death ever so present in the nineteenth century, much interest was shown in mourning samplers. These usually show a weeping willow tree, an urn, a person or two in mourning attire, an appropriately mournful verse, and the deceased's name and dates. Many of these were done on silk and had touches of watercolor as facial features and blue sky. Frequently the center was surrounded by a floral or vining border showing symbolic elements, such as a butterfly for immortality.

COLLECTING TIPS

Seventeenth-century American samplers are extremely rare and will not be found on the market—of course, *anything* is possible, but don't plan on finding one! There were very few made and those documented to exist are in museums. You will find seventeenth-century samplers occasionally, usually at auctions. There seems to be English pieces of that period in America, and they are difficult to distinguish from American pieces. Usually the English show much better workmanship because the teachers were more demanding; frequently the motifs will be strictly English and wool foundations were sometimes used. Some early American samplers will have a crown in the design, making it all the more difficult to document.

Part of the enjoyment of collecting samplers is researching the families of these young ladies who made them. It is possible to check back through old church records, wills, inventories, and old publications to document your sampler. Most samplers were signed, and many had the maker's town, school name or headmistress's name and date, making a search back into the history of their lives a very interesting hobby.

Although samplers were made in America from the time of the late sixteenth century, the most frequently seen on the market today will be from the nineteenth century up to the latter part of the Victorian era. When public schools became available, it was no longer necessary for girls to learn their alphabet by doing samplers. The designs soon lost their original purpose and became just pretty handmade pictures to hang on the wall, not pictures for the study of stitches and designs. Indelible ink became available and household linens did not require the painstaking stitches to mark the numbers and initials. We lost a beautiful and exciting tradition. Although there is a renewed interest in making samplers today, usually from kits, they will never equal the naiveté and freshness of those made by young schoolgirls of long ago.

Some collecting tips to remember are:

• Early samplers were long and narrow, many not having a border but horizontal designs, as in band samplers.

• In the eighteenth century, samples began to grow shorter and wider, almost making a square. These soon became more rectangular, but not as slim as the earlier types.

• Look for Adam and Eve appearing in the mid-eighteenth century. They stay popular until the early nineteenth century. Of course, no pattern or motif completely died out on a given date; many continued for some time, but that was the period of greatest popularity.

• Most of the early band samplers had only alphabets and numbers. Frequently they were not hemmed because horizontal strips were sometimes added onto them as the girl learned more stitches or practiced additional patterns.

• Early nineteenth-century samplers began showing stylized trees, houses, and vining borders. The vining strawberry was a very popular form and usually found only on American samplers.

• From the early nineteenth century on, look for additions of verses included in the design, as well as larger samplers with pictorial designs where the entire open space of the sampler is filled with motifs that the maker loved. A girl from a farm might have her sampler filled with farm animals; some may have just flowers and perhaps a bird or two; many had lambs, goats, and sheep that were suggested by some of the patterns available in the schools. So many of these are so original and show so much spontaneity and freshness that they are completely charming and disarming. (As you may gather from this, pictorials are rather exciting to me.)

• Always check the sampler out of the frame. An original always has a very narrow hem all around. Material was dear and no one ever put in a wide hem.

• If the sampler is original and has been in a frame, the back will have fresh colors while the front will show the proper amount of fading from exposure to light.

• A sampler which has been framed will frequently show nail holes in the border, usually with a little rust around the holes. If not nail holes, there will be small holes from a needle where the sampler was fastened to a backing before being framed.

• Considering backings, many samplers which were framed were laid down on the wood backing or a piece of cardboard. This was deadly. It was not known then that wood contained acids which would destroy the fabrics and threads. Glue was even worse.

• If the cardboard was not acid-free, it most probably has burned through to the fabric. I have seen valuable samplers which had the wood back of the frame touching the fabric, and the grain pattern of the wood had burned through to the front of the sampler, damaging the value of a precious piece of our history.

• Unfortunately, some samplers have been laid down with glue. If it is the old, yellow mucilage type which has dried, it is possible to very gently remove the sampler from the glue and backing. This is a tedious process requiring an Exacto blade and many hours of patience which is better left to an expert. If, unfortunately, someone has used a modern synthetic glue, forget it. It is there to stay. Again, consult an expert—it is your last resort. *Check for glue. Always examine a sampler out of the frame.*

• Older samplers will show threads on the back that have knots; some will show loose threads and will transfer from one design to the other without tying off. If the foundation fabric is thin, the transferring threads may be visible through to the front. The sampler was supposed to be handsome and perfect from the front—no one was supposed to view the reverse except the maker. If the sampler has merit, this will not reduce the value.

• Never try to date the sampler by the style and age of the frame. Samplers were seldom framed at the time of stitching, except in the case of especially involved renditions which the family had framed and hung in the front parlor to show off to their friends and acceptable suitors. Some parents were inclined to make a social production out of the education of their daughter. They went to great lengths to have her play the piano, recite poetry, and show her sampler for all to see at gatherings intended just for that purpose. Many engravings of the period lampoon this practice, and these are very collectible.

• When Empire furniture was popular in this country (early to mid-nineteenth century), sampler designs showed the same influence of larger sizes with heavier designs.

• Late Victorian designs will not show the original purpose of the sampler and will have a pattern of just a pretty picture to hang on a wall.

• It is important to check for the age of the fabrics and threads used. Many reproductions have been made using tea to age the appearance of the sampler. Check Fibers in the "Glossary" to determine the fibers used and if they are homespun as represented. Early samplers with wool threads will show wear to the designs; silks will also show thinning and will almost disappear in some of the designs. Look for wear to the surface of the fabric. Old fabric will feel soft rather than crisp, as with newer fabric. Some reproductions will have been artificially faded and this will show on the back as well as the front.

Research, research, research! Visit shops, auctions, estate sales, tag sales, antiques shows, and flea markets. Many of the less expensive samplers are found in the most unexpected places because, as with lace, too few people are aware of the true value of what they have to sell. We never know when we will find a treasure!

QUALITY AND
CONDITION KEYS

CONDITION KEYS

Measures only the physical condition of the article and not the quality of design, material or workmanship.

Fine Condition (FC): As near mint as possible. There should be no holes or tears in the foundation. Edges intact; colors are bright for age and mellowed properly. Minor repairs executed in a professional manner. No losses of threads or only minor losses.

Good Condition (GC): Few repairs that are not too obvious. Fabric and colors aged properly for period; no stains; no thin areas. Clean.

Average Condition (AC): Some repairs, minor fading, slight thinning; minor spot; may need cleaning. This is the condition in which samplers are most often found.

Poor Condition (PC): Thin foundation with tears or holes; frayed edges; losses; fading; soiled. Not collectible for investment. Depending upon date and important provenance, may be collectible as an interesting piece if restored and framed by a professional.

QUALITY KEYS

Measures the stylishness and collectibility of the piece within its category.

Good Quality (GQ): Attractive piece worthy of collecting, but not for investment.

Very Good Quality (VGQ): Visually attractive; colors and design well defined; well executed; all elements stylistically correct for period.

Superior Quality (SQ): Artistically stunning; design well executed; expert workmanship; all elements are superb and of the period.

MARKET TRENDS

At this time, the market is rather stable. You will note that of the three samplers in the listing section which were sold by Christie's, New York, two important pieces sold below the pre-sale estimates. The market seems to be leveling off after an earlier wild time in the 1980s. Decorators found samplers to be very exciting in their business and collectors became enamored as though they had not been seen before—between the two, prices were pushed up at auction duels. This sort of excitement always turns on the general public and prices realized went out of the ceiling.

Fortunately, today the market seems to be more in line with the values of the merchandise. From my research and the values that I have been able to document, there are a few very acceptable samplers still available in the four-figure and less range. These would make a very exciting foundation for a starting collection, or a suitable addition to one that has been established and needs a little fresh material.

There are many samplers coming out of estates and grandmothers' trunks to keep the prices in line with the public demand for beauty at affordable prices. So now, hopefully, they will not all go to museums, and especially not to private collections, where they would never see the light of day again as far as the public is concerned.

CARING FOR
AND DISPLAYING
YOUR SAMPLERS

Samplers are textiles and must be treated and cared for as with all other textiles mentioned in this book. They are fragile and are susceptible to moisture, mildew, moths, dust, exposure to sunlight, fluorescent lighting, and all other ills which we guard against in other textiles. In caring for and displaying your samplers, therefore, remember the following:

• Never store a sampler in plastic; it will hold moisture and cause mildew and rot.

• They should never be hung in direct sunlight or where they will be exposed to fluorescent lighting. This causes fading.

• Exposure to a source of heat or air-conditioning will result in mildew and rot.

• Protect from common house dust. Dust contains acids that will fade and rot fabrics. Always display under glass for protection.

• Never store in an attic or basement. The extremes of heat and dampness or moisture will cause mildew and rot.

• The only cleaning I would advise, other than sending to an expert, is to cover the sampler with a piece of cheesecloth a few inches larger in dimension, weigh down the outer edges, and hold a vacuum about two inches from the surface, using the most gentle suction available. Never allow the vacuum to touch the fabric. It will take out fragile threads and tear the foundation.

• Because the threads and yarns are usually colored with homemade vegetable dyes and will run and bleed, do not attempt to do any cleaning without testing every color and type of thread used. Unless you are an expert, I would strongly advise seeking the services of an expert in the field of textile conservation. It simply is not worth the chance of destroying something that old and valuable.

• When framing, seek the advice of an expert. The sampler must never touch the glass or any backing except acid-free material. Cardboard and wood contain acids that will cause staining through to the face of the sampler and destroy the fabric and threads.

• Before framing, the sampler must be stitched to a backing of acid-free fabric; the fabric should be several inches larger on all four sides. Using an acid-free board, turn the excess fabric to the back and stitch together to hold the sampler taut on the front. When placing in the frame, all areas of wood must be covered with acid-free material and an inner lining must be placed in the cove so that the glass never touches the fabric of the sampler. At this point, a backing should be placed on and fastened into place with small nails or glazer's points. The stitching on the back of the lining fabric does not need to be fancy; it is only holding the sampler in place and will not be viewed once it is in the frame. If in doubt, consult an expert!

SAMPLERS LISTING

Alphabet 9⅝″ × 10″   Ca. 1820   United States
Homespun. Alphabet, and "Berry Toghill worked this in her 7th year." Blue floss on natural linen. Framed. GQ/AC   *$324.50 (A)* .... $250–$450
Alphabet 11″ × 12½″   1821   United States
Homespun linen. Alphabets, vining border, crown, and "Mary Glynn 1821." Shades of brown, green, and white. Framed. GQ/AC   *$179.30 (A)*. $100–$300
Alphabet 19″ × 17½″   1857   United States
On homespun. Rows of alphabet, and "Sarah Alecksandrien—January 24, 1857." Colors are faded and minor strains. Framed. (This sampler came with a hand-written French birth certificate for the same girl [spelling of Alexandrine differs], dated 1845; stains, matted and framed, 13½″ × 11½″.) GQ/AC   *$424.50 Both (A)* .... $350–$500
Alphabet 8½″ wide × 18″ high   1830   United States
On homespun. Floral border with rows of alphabet, and "Sarah Carmack's work done in the 14th year of her age, 1830." Linen is dark with minor stains and has one hole. Silk floss has faded. Framed. GQ/AC   *$495 (A)* .... $350–$600
Alphabet 17¾″ × 11½″   1785   United States
On homespun. Vining border, alphabets, bird, and "Elizabeth Fearby Acomb." Wear, fading, holes, and missing floss. FQ/PC   *$632.50 (A)* .... $300–$900

> Even though this is in poor condition, quality and age determined the value.

The CONDITION KEY measures only the physical condition of the article and not the quality of design, material or workmanship.
Fine Condition (FC): As near mint as possible. There should be no holes or tears in the foundation. Edges intact; colors are bright for age and mellowed properly. Minor repairs executed in a professional manner. No losses of threads or only minor losses.
Good Condition (GC): Few repairs that are not too obvious. Fabric and colors aged properly for period; no stains; no thin areas. Clean.
Average Condition (AC): Some repairs, minor fading, slight thinning; minor spots; may need cleaning. This is the condition in which samplers are most often found.
Poor Condition (PC): Thin foundation with tears or holes; frayed edges; losses; fading; soiled. Not collectible for investment. Depending upon date and important provenance, may be collectible as an interesting piece if restored and framed by a professional.

The QUALITY KEY measures the stylishness and collectibility of the piece within its category.
Good Quality (GQ): Attractive piece worthy of collecting, but not for investment.
Very Good Quality (VGQ): Visually attractive; colors and design well defined; well executed; all elements stylistically correct for period.
Superior Quality (SQ): Artistically stunning; design well executed; expert workmanship; all elements are superb and of the period.

Alphabet   18½″ × 10¼″   Ca. 1820–1830   United States
On homespun. Colorful alphabets, house, trees, birds, etc., in cross stitch and
needlepoint. Minor floss loss and small mended holes at chimney. Framed. GQ/
GC *$550 (A)* .... $350–$650

Alphabet and Verse   13¾″ × 11½″   1774   Norwich, Connecticut
Worked in green, blue, rose, and white silk and metal threads, on a black ground
with bands of alphabets and numerals embellished with carnations, flowers, and
Greek key bands. Inscribed with verse: "Who can find a virtuous woman. For her
price is far above rubies," above a scene depicting a shepherdess with a flock of
sheep and a house with palm and fruit trees. Inscribed below: "Alice Mather, her
sampler made in the twelvth year of her age July th 8 AD 1774." Silk ground fabric
sewn to an original chintz border with a vine and berry decoration (slightly faded).
(See photo 154) SQ/FC   *$49,500 (A)* .... $50,000–$80,000

> When a fine and rare sampler such as this example comes to auction, it is
> very difficult to place a sliding scale of value other than the estimates given
> by the auction company. Such exquisite workmanship and condition do not
> come to light very often today! This obviously was kept stored away for it to
> remain in such pristine condition. *Remember—condition is extremely impor-*
> *tant.*

PHOTO 154

PHOTO CREDIT: CHRISTIE'S, NY

Alphabet and Verse 14¼″ × 12½″ 1765 Massachusetts
Homespun linen. Worked in green, blue, purple, yellow, and white silk threads.
Alphabet flanked by bands of strawberry and geometric designs above verse:
"On Earth Let May Example Shine and When I Leave this State May Heaven
Relieve this Soul of Mine to this Devinely Great," above a pastoral scene of a
lady and gentleman with a flock of sheep and a bird over an inscription "Sarah
Doubt wrought this sampler in the 10 year of her Ae 1765." The whole flanked
by vines and strawberries (slight fading). *(See photo 155)* SQ/FC *$6,655 (A)*
.... $8,000–$12,000

> This is another early sampler in excellent condition, although it did not quite
> reach the pre-sale estimate. It was a good buy for the purchaser and worthy
> for any collection.

Family Record 20″ × 27½″ 1831 United States
On linen homespun. Family record with geometric and foliage border. Recorded
are births and two deaths in the Howlet family. Signed "Mary Howlet aged 12"
(she was born in 1819). Stains and several small holes. Colors are a bit faded.
Framed. GQ/AC *$137.50 (A)* .... $125–$300
Family Record 17¾″ × 17¾″ Ca. 1820 United States
On linen homespun. Family record with floral border. Recorded are births and
two deaths in the Collins family (last recorded date is 1845). Colors are a bit
faded. Old gilt frame. GQ/AC *$165 (A)* .... $125–$300
Miniature 7¾″ × 6¾″ and 8½″ × 7″ Ca. 1820 United States
Two, on homespun. Needlepoint and other stitches in lovely old faded colors.
Bird on branch, pot of flowers, and a castle with tree and figure. All have stains
and holes in homespun. Original black reeded frames with old glass. GQ/
PC *$990 Set (A)* .... $600–$1,200 Set
Mourning 31¼″ × 29½″ 1870 Bury, England
Memorial to Edward and Molley Peers with floral border, tomb, and "Molley
Peer's work, aged 12 yrs. Bury, 1870." Foundation is stained, but wool yarn has
retained good color. Framed. GQ/PC *$115.50 (A)* .... $100–$300
Pictorial 23½″ × 24″ 1832 Springfield, Ohio
On linen homespun. Vining strawberry border, with flowers, building, verses,
alphabets, and "Hannah Haas's work, Jan 13 1832." The 1860 census listed
Hannah Haas as born in Pennsylvania in 1815 and working at Springfield, Ohio,
Female Academy. Shades of brown, green, and blue with other colors. Some
fading and wear, with floss missing in several flowers and damage along top
edge. Matted and framed. SQ/GC *$2,475 (A)* .... $1,500–$3,000
Pictorial 17½″ × 12½″ 1796 United States
Worked in polychrome, with an alphabetic sequence above an inscription from
Proverbs over birds and floral motifs. Inscription: "Mary Ewing sewed this sam-
pler in the year 1796." *(See photo 156)* VGQ/FC *$1,028.50 (A)* .... $300–$500
Pictorial 22½″ × 19½″ 1850 Bath, Maine
On homespun. Vining border with stylized flowers and architectural detail with
deer, birds, building, verse, and "Elizabeth Bartlett aged 10 April 16, 1850,
York Street Chapel Day School, Bath." Wear, small holes, and homespun is
puckering; colors have bled. Shadowbox frame. GQ/AC *$770 (A)* ....
.... $500–$1,000
Pictorial 14½″ × 15½″ 1785 United States
Finely woven cotton homespun. Small precise stitches with stylized flowers,
birds, animals, crowns, and central tree with two figures. "M.D. 1785." Good

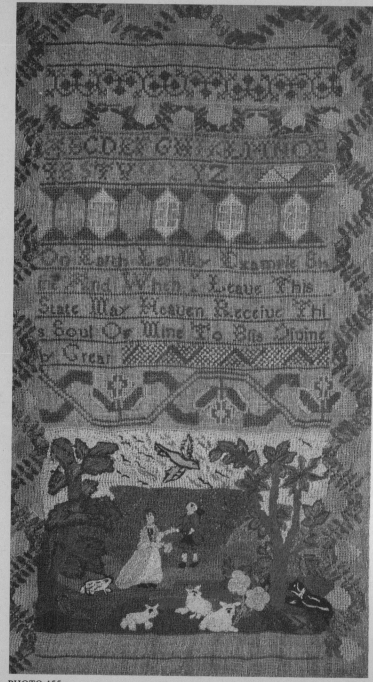

PHOTO 155

PHOTO CREDIT: CHRISTIE'S, NY

PHOTO 156

color with red, blue, green, yellow, white, and brown. Several small holes in homespun and some floss is worn. Matted and bird's-eye maple frame. GQ/GC *$770 (A)* .... $500–$900

Verse 13¾″ × 18¼″ 1824 United States
On linen homespun. Rows of alphabets, numerals, verse, stylized flowers, and "Mary Pratt finished this sampler May 26th, 1824 in the ninth year of her age." Red floss. Minor stains and a small hole. Framed. VGQ/GC *$605 (A)*..........
.... $450–$700

Verse 17″ × 15″ 1825 United States
On linen homespun. Five styles of alphabets and numbers. One row with eyelet-worked letters. Linen has darkened and floss has faded to shades of brown; some losses. Verse: ". . . I live. Live while you live the epicure wold [*sic*] say, and seize the pleasures of the day, Live while you live the preacher cries, And give unto God each moment as it flies," in faded black and red. Signed by Saloma Small, 1825. Not framed. GQ/PC *$115 (D)*............................. $100–$300

Verse 14½″ × 15¾″ 1792 United States
On homespun linen, finely woven. Well-executed floral border in colorful silk floss, and "Psalm LXVIII, . . . Betty Cully her work February 22, 1792." Worn, holes, and floss is missing in verse. Framed. GQ/PC *$275 (A)*...........
.... $200–$400

MUSEUMS

There are many fine museums around the country that have collections of samplers; those listed below are just a small representation. Always check ahead before visiting a museum because the display which you are interested in may not be open to the public when you arrive.

Chester County Historical Society
Westchester, PA

Cooper-Hewitt Museum
Smithsonian's National Museum of Design
New York, NY

Henry Francis Du Pont Winterthur Museum
Winterthur, DE

Metropolitan Museum of Art
New York, NY

Museum of American Folk Art
New York, NY

Whitney Museum of American Art
New York, NY

BIBLIOGRAPHY

Bishop, Robert, William Secord, and Judith Reiter Weissman. *Quilts, Coverlets, Rugs and Samplers*. New York: E.P. Dutton & Co., Inc., 1982.

Harbeson, Georgiana Brown. *American Needlework: History of Decorative Stitchery and Embroidery From the Late 16th to the 20th Century*. New York: Coward-McCann, 1938; New York: Bonanza Books, 1961.

Krueger, Glee F. *A Gallery of American Samplers: The Theodore Kapnek Collection*. New York: E.P. Dutton & Co., Inc., in association with the Museum of American Folk Art, 1978.

Ring, Betty. *American Needlework Treasures: Samplers and Silk Embroideries From the Collection of Betty Ring*. New York: E.P. Dutton & Co., Inc., 1987.

Appendixes

APPENDIX A:
APPRAISAL SOCIETIES

The reputation and value of appraisal societies are becoming more important to the public because of new tax laws and new demands for testing and certification of appraisers by government (to satisfy IRS nationally) and by individual state requirements. Listed here are the only two appraisal societies that demand attendance at multidisciplinary classes presented at various times of the year in various parts of the country. Every member of each of these societies must pass rigorous examinations and must recertify every five years to stay abreast of the market and the many applicable tax laws. Both societies place great stress on Personal Property discipline.

American Society of Appraisers
International Headquarters
P.O. Box 17265
Washington, DC 20041

This organization was established over fifty years ago. It tests rigorously and certifies on two levels—Member and Senior Member. Brochures are available to the public at no cost by writing to the above address.

International Society of Appraisers
P.O. Box 726
Hoffman Estates, IL 60195

This society was organized about fourteen years ago. It also demands courses and testing. It offers a broad range of educational advantages, including degree courses through Indiana University, all available to the public at a fee. Contact ISA at the above address.

APPENDIX B:
DEALER ORGANIZATIONS

Regarding dealer organizations, there are small groups and statewide organizations, some of which have a few members around the country. There are a few that exist to lobby, and another few that present educational programs and are social. However, there is only one large, inclusive, dealer organization in the United States.

The National Association of Dealers in Antiques, Inc., is an association which is national in scope and provides many educational advantages as well as scholarships.

National Association of Dealers in Antiques, Inc.
P.O. Box 421
Barrington, IL 60011
Phone: (312) 381–7096

This organization was founded in 1961 and stresses a code of ethics in business which is very strict. You may contact the office above if you would like to receive material or if you are in the antiques business and would like to have information about becoming a member.

There is a wonderful network among members around the country which is valuable for the interchange of education and information. National seminars are held in conjunction with Kent State University and are offered twice a year. NADA offers a scholarship of $3,000 annually to the Cooper-Hewitt Museum graduate program in the History of Decorative Arts.

Membership is open to show and shop dealers, educators in the antiques field, auction houses, show managers, and publishers in the antiques field. If you are not in any of these categories, contact the national office and ask to be notified of the national educational programs which non-members may be invited to attend.

APPENDIX C: RESTORATIONISTS

One of the most important considerations of textile care is the service of a professional conservationist who is scientifically trained in museum work and dealing with fine collections. There are specialists in many areas of the country, and most museums will help with information in locating someone for your needs. Three of the major firms who are qualified in this area are listed below.

Each of these firms has very instructive brochures which you may receive by calling or writing to the addresses below. Always contact the firm for information concerning your particular needs before shipping any material to them.

Bryce Reveley Gentle Arts
P.O. Box 15832
New Orleans, LA 70113
Telephone: (504) 895-5628
Complete antique textile
service and appraising.

Chevalier Conservation
500 West Avenue
Stamford, CT 06902
Telephone: (203) 969–1980
Fax: (203) 969–1988

M. Finkel & Daughter
936 Pine Street
Philadelphia, PA 19107
Telephone: (215) 627-7797

The Textile Conservation Workshop, Inc.
Main Street
South Salem, NY 10590
Telephone: (914) 763–5805
The executive director and founder of
this nonprofit and tax-exempt organization
is Patsy Orlofsky, known to many as an
authority on 19th-century American
textiles, author, and lecturer.

APPENDIX D:
AUCTION HOUSES

These houses usually have some textiles listed in their catalogs. Christie's, New York, and Sotheby's, New York, both have important decorative arts sales in January of each year. These sales usually set the course for the coming season. Garth's has a sale almost every month and always has textiles; these are not quite as dear as those found in the New York houses and thus can be very attractive as well as affordable.

Christie's, New York
502 Park Avenue
New York, NY 10022

Garth's Auctions, Inc.
2690 Stratford Road
P.O. Box 369
Delaware, OH 43015

Sotheby's
1334 York Avenue
New York, NY 10021

Catalogs may be purchased from each of these houses. You may select your category of interest and receive a catalog in advance, as well as a list of sales results for reference.

APPENDIX E: PERIODICALS

Many of these publications have articles and references to textiles.

Antique Monthly
c/o Boone, Inc.
P.O. Drawer 2
Tuscaloosa, AL 35401

Antiques and Arts Weekly
c/o The Newtown Bee
Newtown, CT 06470

Antiques Magazine, The
551 Fifth Avenue
New York, NY 10017

Art & Antiques
89 Fifth Avenue
New York, NY 10003

Carolina Antique News
P.O. Box 241114
Charlotte, NC 28224

Country Living Magazine
224 W. 57th Street
New York, NY 10019

Early American Life
2245 Kohn Road
P.O. Box 8200
Harrisburg, PA 17105–8200

Maine Antique Digest
P.O. Box 645
Waldoboro, ME 04572

Mid-Atlantic Antiques Magazine
P.O. Box 908
Henderson, NC 27536

Traditional Home
Meredith Corp.
1716 Locust Street
Des Moines, IA 50336

West Coast Peddler
P.O. Box 5134
Whittier, CA 90607

GLOSSARY

Album Quilt. The practice of incorporating many differing patterns; frequently each done by a different person. Usually an appliqué quilt. Best example: "Baltimore" quilts, dating between 1846–1852.

Analine Dye. Synthetic dyes developed in the late nineteenth century. Very bright as opposed to vegetable dyes. They do not fade into soft shades as with vegetable dyes.

Antimacassar. Refers to a doily designed to be placed on the back of a chair in the late nineteenth century to protect it from macassar, an oily hairdressing used by men. Most sets had arm rests as well.

Appenzell. Beautiful embroidery and drawn work using pale blue thread on fine linen, and now cotton. Appenzell was a canton in Switzerland, now divided.

Appliqué. A piece of fabric cut into a form and stitched onto another fabric.

Backing. The bottom side piece of fabric on a quilt.

Baste. To sew with long loose stitches to hold fabrics together; removed after permanent stitching.

Batiste. A soft, thin, cotten muslin fabric, used for baby clothes, blouses, handkerchiefs, and any other items requiring a soft thin fabric.

Batting. Usually of cotton wool or other fibers used as an inner lining for warmth in a quilt.

Bed Furniture. Refers to the necessary covers and hangings for the bed in early America, not the bed itself.

Bed Rug. A hooked rug used on the bed as a cover. Each was individually designed by the maker, usually showing name or initials and date. Majority of all extant today are in museums. The probability of ever finding one on the market is quite remote.

Berlin Work. Needlework done on printed canvas or by printed patterns, usually originating in Berlin in the nineteenth century. The patterns often came with the wool yarns. Today the printed, hand-colored graph patterns are highly collectible and are very attractive when framed.

Binding. A narrow piece of fabric used to edge a quilt or a hooked rug.

Block. Usually a square used in making a patchwork quilt.

Braided Rug. Made from strips of wool or cotton fabric, and from worn clothing in a variety of materials. Braided and stitched together to form a floor covering.

Calico. A cotton fabric printed in small patterns, usually in two colors. Originated in Calcutta; introduced into England and finally to America.

Cambric. Originated with the French in the town of Cambria. A thin and delicate linen, it now refers to a cotton muslin.

Candlewicking. Usually on a bedspread; a running stitch made from heavy cotton thread used for candlewicks. It formed a raised pile pattern which was sometimes clipped. It was popular in the early to mid-nineteenth century. Machine-made reproductions were popular in the mid-twentieth century, often using colors.

Canvas. Derived from the Latin *cannabis*, a hemp. A heavy cloth used for tents, sails, upholstery, and background fabric for needlepoint.

Challis. A thin twilled fabric made from wool and silk originally. Now made of synthetics and a variety of other fibers. It is printed in many different colors and patterns.

Chintz. Color-fast printed fabric which has been glazed. Used mostly for household furnishings.

Cochineal. Red dyestuff made from the dried bodies of the female cochineal insect, from S. America.

Cotton. See Fibers.

Counterpane. A bedcover, frequently a quilt without middle stuffing; same as bedspread.

Coverlet. A woven bedcover, usually of linen or cotton and wool, in many differing patterns. Popular in the nineteenth century.

Crazy Quilt. A quilt made from many patches of differing materials in irregular shapes. Often had fancy embroidery decorations. Popular in the late nineteenth century.

Crewelwork. Needlework done with two-ply, loosely twisted wool yarn. Usually on linen in patterns of free-flowing flowers and vines. In early America, the color was mostly shades of blue.

Crib Quilt. A smaller version of a full-size quilt; scaled-down patterns were used for children's beds.

Damask. A twilled material with ornamental designs, in relief, woven into the fabric. Used mostly for furniture, except the damask linens which were used for table appointments.

Diaper. A figured cloth, woven in diamond-shaped designs. Used for towels and other household furnishings, as well as for baby napkins. Woven of linen or cotton in Ireland and Scotland originally.

Dimity. A cotton fabric woven with double threads in raised designs of stripes or cross-bars. Some may be printed. Used for bed hangings and other household furnishings. In early days, used for women's petticoats.

Doily. A small cloth or mat, usually decorative.

Dotted Swiss. A lightweight cotton fabric with woven thread dots in an all-over pattern.

Double Damask. Same as damask, but woven to be reversible.

Double-weave Coverlet. A coverlet made with two layers woven simultaneously; the layers are interwoven where the pattern changes. Also referred to as "double-cloth" coverlet.

Embroidery. The art of decorating a fabric by using a needle and a variety of threads, including cotton, silk, wool, gold, silver, and synthetics. Uses a variety of stitches. It is considered the first depiction of natural objects in their natural colors, and dates back to antiquity.

Face. The top side or front of a textile meant to be viewed.

Faggoting. A design gained by removing rows of weft threads and then tying groups of the remaining warp threads together in an hourglass figure.

Fibers. Fibers used in textiles are long, thin, and strong enough to be woven. These fibers may be animal, mineral, vegetable or manmade.

TYPES OF FIBERS

Animal: Animal fibers are protein and include wool from sheep and from silkworms. Human hair is similar in chemical make-up to wool and was used in the early days of lacemaking for special effects. Silk comes from sources other than silkworms, such as from the spinnerets of spiders and other caterpillars, but neither is strong enough to spin and weave and not plentiful enough for commercial uses.

Mineral: Mineral fibers used in textile making are gold, silver, and metal alloys.

Vegetable: Vegetable fibers are mostly compounded from lignin, although cellulose is also important. The two main sources are cotton and flax. Also included are hemp, jute, and sisal in the manufacture of textiles.

Manmade: Manmade fibers are in two categories:

Regenerated: Fibers made from natural substances, such as rayon from cellulose extracted from wood pulp.

Synthetic: Fibers form polymers. The first to be discovered was a polyamide—nylon. Since then there has been a never-ending stream of new synthetics.

STRUCTURE OF FIBERS

Fibers can be identified by examining the structure with the aid of very strong magnification: cotton is twisted; flax is segmented and appears to be pitted; wool is scaly; and silk and synthetics are long and smooth.

FIBER LENGTHS

Cotton fiber is from .8″ to a maximum of 3″ in length. Flax fiber runs to approximately 36″ in length. Wool is found up to 8″ in length. Silk commonly runs to 1,950 feet for a single thread. Synthetics run to infinity.

TESTING FOR IDENTIFICATION BY BURNING

Animal protein fibers: wool and silk will smell like singeing hair and then go out, leaving black charcoal. Plant fibers: cotton and flax will burn immediately without an odor, leaving no ash. Silk and synthetics: will melt and then burn.

IDENTIFICATION BY THICKNESS OF FIBER

Usually cotton is thicker than flax, wool is thicker than cotton, and silk fiber is the thinnest. Synthetics can be whatever is required for the intended use.

Foundation. The base fabric on which a sampler or rug is stitched. Usually of a loosely woven cloth.

Fringe, Wedding Knots. Fringe is the tying off of the loose warp threads into a decorative edging. Wedding knots refers to double or triple knotting of the threads into a trellis pattern.

Gingham. A cotton fabric with two or more colors woven in a design of checks or stripes.

Hawaiian Quilt. Made in Hawaii in the nineteenth century of appliqués of native fruits, flowers, and frequently the flag. Very intricately cut and quilted.

Hemstitch. Similar to faggoting, but not as deep and without intricate designs.

Homespun. A loosely hand-woven fabric, usually of linen or wool hand-spun yarns.

Hooked Rug. A floor covering made from strips of fabrics hooked through a foundation of loosely woven linen or hemp.

Huck, Huck-a-back. A coarse kind of linen cloth manufactured with small knots over the surface making a rough face. Used mostly for towels. May also be made of cotton or a mixture of both.

Indigo Dye. A dark blue vegetable dye from the indigo plant. Originally from India; became an important crop in the South, especially South Carolina. Now a less expensive synthetic is used.

Jacquard Coverlet. A large coverlet woven on a loom with a special mechanized attachment. Look for curvilinear, often representational, designs and an intricate border.

Linen. See Fibers.

Linsey-woolsey. A coarse fabric woven with cotton or linen warp and wool weft. Frequently it is glazed. Used for rough clothing and bed-covers.

Madder. An herb from Asia where the root is used for dye, which is a moderate to strong red.

Marseilles Spread. A bedcover woven by a process which resembles white-on-white hand-quilted and stuffed work. Machine was invented in Marseilles, France, in the nineteenth century. Many are still available for collecting.

Mercerized Cotton. Cotton thread which has been treated with a chemical and spun to a fine, tight, smooth, silky thread. This process made the thread much stronger than before, while still being very thin. It was invented ca. 1850 and introduced commercially in 1890. It was intended to replace silk for making lace and for fine sewing. The trade name was "Sylko."

Merrow. A machine edging on fabric, somewhat resembling a single-crocheted edge. Often seen on machine-made tablecloths and napkins.

Mull. A fine, soft, white muslin originally used for women's mourning dresses, and children's and babies' clothes.

Muslin. A thin, more or less transparent cotton textile. It is named for the town of Moosul in Turkey. Muslin was introduced into England via India ca. 1670, and then to America. It is made in many different weights and qualities. Unbleached muslin is a light cream color and must be pre-shrunk before using.

Natural Dye. A dye extracted from plants, nuts or animal material.

Needlework Picture. A decorative textile made on a foundation of linen or silk using linen, silk, wool or sometimes metallic threads to depict various scenes of mourning, biblical or homeplace designs. Frequently watercolor was used for portions of the picture.

Overshot Coverlet. A bedcover in which some of the weft threads overshoot three or more warp threads to create a simple pattern. The warp is usually linen or cotton and the weft is wool. They were made on a narrow loom and seamed in the middle.

Palampore. A cotton spread, richly colored, frequently with the Tree of Life pattern in the center. It came from India to England in the eighteenth century.

Percale. A cotton fabric of fine silky texture, frequently woven 200–300 threads to the inch. Used for fine quality beddings.

Pieced. Pieces of fabric sewn together at the edges to form a solid textile, such as a quilt top.

Pile. Loops on the surface of fabric, either cut or uncut, to create a raised finish by projecting through the surface, such as velvet.

Pillow Sham. A decorative linen or cotton cover placed over bed pillows during the day when the bed is not in use. They can be of envelope or single-layer throw type.

Pima. A long staple cotton grown in Pima, Arizona. It has been developed by hybridization or natural selection from Egyptian cotton and is considered to be of finest quality.

Plain Weave. The simplest form of woven textile where one weft passes over one warp thread, alternately, producing a plain woven surface.

Provenance. The history of a textile where ownership is traced back to its origin.

Quilting. The stitches which bind the three layers of a quilt together, often in a decorative manner.

Rag Rug. A floor covering woven from strips of rags of various fibers—cotton, wool, etc.

Rayon. See Fibers.

Resist Dyeing. A method of decorating fabric in which the pattern not receiving the dye has been waxed over before immersion. The wax is then removed, leaving that area undyed and creating a design.

Reverse Appliqué. A technique where a portion of the appliqué is removed, exposing the foundation fabric through the design.

Ruffle. A strip of fabric which has been gathered on one edge and stitched to produce a decorative flounce trim.

Sampler. A decorative needlework embroidered to show a variety of stitches, usually including the alphabet and numbers, some with verses and biblical reference. Most are signed or initialed and dated. The majority have been worked by schoolgirls to use as samples for later stitchery.

Sashes. The strips or blocks that separate the squares in a quilt top. Also called ''Sets.''

Satin Stitch. An embroidery stitch where the design is worked over a felt underlay to create a bas relief of the design.

Seersucker. Originally a Persian fabric called ''shir-o-shakar'' (milk and honey), a blister-puckered and plain-weave stripe. The name was simplified for the western world. Now used for clothing, household furnishings, and many other uses.

Selvage, Selvedge. The edge of the fabric which has been woven to prevent fraying (corruption of self-edge).

Sets. Same as Sashes, which see.

Shirred Rug. An arrangement of thickly ruffled strips of fabric which has been stitched down onto a foundation of burlap or linen. The strips are often cut on the bias. This process makes a pile surface rug depending upon the width of the ruffles.

Silk. See Fibers.

Sizing. A glutinous substance used for filling pores in the surface of textiles (and other materials) to create a stiffening or thickening of the fabric. It will wash out in the first laundering, leaving the fabric limp.

Stuffed Work. A quilt design stuffed from the back to make the pattern stand out puffy.

Summer Spread. Usually a quilt without filling and sometimes without backing used as a bedcover.

Summer/winter Coverlet. A woven coverlet with the design reversible, dark on one side and light on the other. Supposedly the light side was used in summer and the dark in winter.

Template. A pattern made of cardboard, paper or tin used to trace a design to make an accurate cutting for a quilt top or designing a rug.

Trapunto. A type of stuffed work occasionally found on American quilts. After a design is quilted, a cord is inserted to give a raised, stuffed-like appearance. Originated in Italy.

Tucks. Rows of finely stitched folded areas which are pressed flat on the face of the fabric.

Tufting. Stitched threads coming through from the bottom to the top of the three layers of a quilt and knotted in areas close enough to hold the layers and prevent shifting.

Valance. A short drapery used at the top of a bed hanging or window to conceal the structural element.

Warp. The longitudinal threads in textiles.

Weave. To form cloth on a loom by running horizontal weft threads over and under longitudinal warp threads.

Weft. The horizontal threads in textiles.

White Work Spread. Any spread that is decorated with white threads on a white ground.

Wool. See Fibers.

Worsted. A smooth compact yarn of long wool fibers used to weave fabrics and rugs and for knitting.

Yarn-sewn Rug. A floor covering made by sewing yarn in a continuous running stitch on a tightly woven foundation and leaving loops on the surface to form a pile. Frequently the loops are clipped.

INDEX